TWENTIETH CENTURY INTERPRETATIONS

OF

A TALE OF TWO CITIES

TWENTIETH CENTURY INTERPRETATIONS
OF

A TALE OF
TWO CITIES

A Collection of Critical Essays
Edited by
CHARLES E. BECKWITH

Prentice-Hall, Inc. *Englewood Cliffs, N. J.*

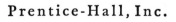

A SPECTRUM BOOK

PRENTICE-HALL INTERNATIONAL, INC. (*London*)
PRENTICE-HALL OF AUSTRALIA, PTY. LTD. (*Sydney*)
PRENTICE-HALL OF CANADA, LTD. (*Toronto*)
PRENTICE-HALL OF INDIA PRIVATE LTD. (*New Delhi*)
PRENTICE-HALL OF JAPAN, INC. (*Tokyo*)

Contents

Contents

Introduction

by Charles E. Beckwith

"I hope it is the best story I have written," wrote Dickens on finishing *A Tale of Two Cities*; and elsewhere, "Heaven knows I have done my best and believed in it." [1] Such defensiveness reflects the special circumstances that preceded the writing of this book, and the special struggles that they led to. For one thing, he had undertaken a new magazine, *All the Year Round*, with himself as both editor and chief contributor, which he planned in weekly parts and intended to open with an eye-catching flourish. He therefore had to organize the novel in tighter segments than usual, with more frequent spots of crisis and suspense. The restriction was painful to the usually expansive Dickens ("the small parts . . . drive me frantic"); and he also, for similar reasons, had trouble with the beginning. The paradoxical patterning of that now-famous passage— "It was the best of times, it was the worst of times, it was the age of wisdom, it was the age of foolishness"—is probably the most noticeable single instance of the forms and devices he worked out to tighten the economy, and speed the movement of the whole. It also, of course, sets a kind of distance between the reader and the events to follow, a distance of the sort that is always caused by the mixing of realism and rhetoric, and that, in a variety of forms, runs through the whole novel—as for example in the monotonous repetition of the word *Hunger* early in the book, in the footsteps and the thunderstorm around the Manettes' house in Soho, in the knitting and the counting of heads at the climax. The necessity of such mixing derives in part from the subject matter, which constitutes another of the special circumstances that Dickens had to contend with in treating this particular story. The French Revolution, being so full of exciting real events all well known to Dickens's readers, was always in effect pulling against his own invention of character, incident, and plot. To make matters worse, Carlyle's famous history, *The French Revolution*, which was Dickens's chief literary inspiration and set the background of historical event and social criticism which he followed in general, was also known to many of Dickens's readers, and was as

---

[1] Letter to Francois Joseph Régnier, October 15, 1859; letter to Wilkie Collins, October 6, 1859, in *The Letters of Charles Dickens*, ed. Walter Dexter (Bloomsbury: The Nonesuch Press, 1938), III, 125.

full of excitement and suspense as any novel of adventure. Dickens stated in his Introduction that no one could "hope to add anything to the philosophy of Mr. Carlyle's wonderful book," and he might have added that no writer of fiction could hope to improve on it in dramatic movement and pictorial brilliancy.

These were some of the special circumstances that occasioned Dickens's struggles with *A Tale of Two Cities.* There were also matters more personal. He was at the very top of his career when he began it and had achieved worldwide fame as a creator of fanciful characters, elaborate and often mysterious plots, and even more elaborate passages of commentary and description, often comic, but equally often sentimental or grotesque; and from the time of his first novel, *Oliver Twist,* he had been also a bold critic of social evils and a prophet of social dangers. But all these strengths had by now shown their obverse side. Fancy and fantasy easily became whimsy; complicated plots and subplots degenerated into forced crises and coincidences; pathos wobbled toward weepiness, as in the famous death of Little Nell in *The Old Curiosity Shop.* In *A Tale of Two Cities,* therefore, Dickens set out determinedly, not to purge the chief characteristics of a lifetime's work (which would have been impossible in any case), but to purge the excesses to which he had often let them run. The result, in the *Tale,* is that we have a plot complicated but fast-moving, stark at times like a Greek tragedy, dispensing with subplot yet managing to weave in surprises, coincidences, and late revelation of the meaning of earlier events. In the double arrest of Charles Darnay, for example, or the ride of the Marquis with his murderer-to-be accompanying him unseen; or again, in the dramatic announcement of Madame Defarge's motivation from years gone by and in her death at the hands of an unexpected but fitting agent—in such moments we have the essential Dickens but distilled to a new quintessence. Similarly, description and background, a great feature of Dickens's, are reduced to functional or symbolic effect, and characterization likewise is minimized; so that perhaps more than with any other novel he wrote, the author himself recedes into the distance, and the story seems to tell itself, or to be unfolding, with only his guidance rather than his usual manipulation.

Such handling of his material appears to have been personally significant to Dickens in the sense that he was showing his audience, and himself, that he could function as well in the art of the novel—better, to judge from the statements quoted above—without the trappings, devices, and lavish coloration of the past. "I set myself," he says,

> the little task of making a *picturesque* story, rising in every chapter, with characters true to nature, but whom the story itself should express, more than they should express themselves, by dialogue.[2]

[2] Letter to John Forster, August 25, 1859, in *Letters,* III, 118.

In the phrase, "I set myself," we see something of the sense of challenge he felt in attempting this particular task, which turned out to be bigger than he had anticipated. There were greater and more personal challenges behind it, too. Critics have often noticed that Dickens's career moves from condemnation of specific social ills, like the workhouse system in *Oliver Twist,* to condemnation of whole corrupt societies, like the mercenary world struggling for a trash heap in *Our Mutual Friend.* In the French Revolution he found a subject worthy of his broadest conceptions: a great nation ripening its own destruction—literally France, of course, but by implication England, too, and any other nation having ingrained feudal privileges with their inherent abuses. The very breadth of that prospect may well be responsible for the deliberate tightening and narrowing of scope in the *Tale.* Avoiding the enormous sweep and drama of the Revolution in all its complexity, he tries to condense the basic threat and the basic lesson by showing the effects of the Terror—the vengeful side of that great event—on a small group of people variously involved.

In a yet more personal way, Dickens's undertaking of this work brings us to the boundary between fact and conjecture. He was going through perhaps the greatest crisis of his life as he approached it, a crisis peculiar in the way it resurrected memories and feelings from earlier crises, making this a compacted period of intense strain. To trace connections between an author's life and his works is always dangerous and uncertain since it plays down the role of the controlling artist; and no work of Dickens's is more controlled. At the same time, the material the artist controls comes, at some stage, from a level of personal experience and feeling; and we can understand better, or be better pointed toward understanding, the finished form of the novel if we look briefly at the roots of some of its themes and their illustrations.

More than most works of Dickens's, this book needs at the present time to be approached thematically. Its special moments and descriptions stand out so unforgettably for most of us—the implacable grimness of Madame Defarge; the sudden upsurge of the mob (a kind of preview of their later quest for blood) when the wine is spilled; the calm heroism, above life and death alike, of Sidney Carton—that they tend to obscure some of the larger and deeper of Dickens's themes—larger and deeper than, for example, social injustice, revolutionary violence, or even individual self-sacrifice. These last, of course, are what the book is "about" in an important sense that we must not slight. But they are obvious themes, themes of statement, themes which lend themselves easily to the merely visual apprehension of its events, hence to the stage and movie career the novel has enjoyed to the detriment of its appreciation as a work of literary art—though, as Dickens's comments make clear, it was as art that he wanted it appreciated. The larger and deeper themes, on the other hand, lead us in more profitable directions. First of all backward—to a view of Dickens's childhood and early life. Then forward—toward a more modern judgment of this strangely "modern" book.

I

We can see the personal themes of Dickens's writing beginning to emerge early in his boyhood, blending with each other in sometimes curious ways, and becoming re-emphasized by later happenings. His first childhood experiences, he makes clear, became associated with dramatic fantasy and rhetoric through his father, who, although a conscientious naval clerk by day, was a kind of Falstaff when off duty, full of elaborate gesture and high-flown speech. One early memory, for example, was of a fine house at Gad's Hill near Rochester, which his father told him he might own, if he worked very hard, when he grew up—an idea with which his imagination continued for a long time to play. Later, these fantasies took on a new dimension when he learned that this was the area where Falstaff had had his night adventures with Prince Hal and the practical jokers who robbed him. Still later—years later—when he accidentally learned of the availability of this house on the market, and bought it and moved there, he felt, as he had so often in his life, the perilous thinness of the boundary between fantasy and fact.

When Dickens was only twelve, another side of the Falstaffian personality—improvidence—sent his father to debtor's prison and left the son to long hours of drudgery in a blacking warehouse. Ever flamboyant, his father remarked when he left for prison: "The sun has set upon me forever!" The son, too, with no way of knowing when or whether he might escape the warehouse, believing indeed that he never would, felt equally lost. More specifically, he felt betrayed by both parents, first by his father for his failure to provide, and later, as if they were taking turns, by his mother for her failure to care what happened to him and to his early talents. As he put it to his friend and later biographer, John Forster, he felt that he, who had been a quick and sensitive and promising student, had been in an instant "thrown away"; and he spoke of his shock when, his father having been released after an unexpected legacy and the question of his own future coming up, he realized that his mother wanted him to stay on indefinitely at the warehouse instead of going back to school: "I never afterwards forgot, I never shall forget, I never can forget, that my mother was warm for my being sent back." [3] He was released, however,

---

[3] These and other details of the prison and warehouse episode, and Dickens's feelings about it, are given by Edgar Johnson in *Charles Dickens: His Tragedy and Triumph*, 2 vols. (New York: Simon and Schuster, Inc., 1952), I, iii, now the standard biography and the chief source of the biographical material in this volume.

and did go back to school, where his former buoyancy and mental agility quickly returned. But his bitterness and sense of betrayal, tinged with the desolate and depressive feelings that the uncared-for child inevitably experiences, remained and were to remain all his life. The whole experience had also given another twist, we can easily conjecture, to his sense of the intermingling of reality and fantasy. Not only were the realities of the occasion so surprising and painful that they had the effect of fantasy—in this case, nightmare—on his childish feelings and imagination; there was also a double betrayal, the falling back from one support to another only to find that too giving away; and there was a confused apprehension of the meaning of what would prove to be one of his repeated overt themes, prison and imprisonment. For he had more reason to feel a prisoner and an outcast than his father did. Life in debtors' prison was a kind of communal arrangement then, and prisoners could have their families with them. John Dickens, always energetic and talkative, soon became the friend and adviser of many of the other prisoners and was made chairman of the committee that provided for their needs. He was an individual and a leader even in those restricted circumstances. Many years later, Charles remembered this anomalous role of his father's when he created William Dorrit, who in *Little Dorrit* served twenty-five years in debtors' prison (Dickens's father served only a few months), and rose to a position that gave him the title—ironic, and perhaps to Dickens bitter in memory—of "master of the Marshalsea." Charles, meanwhile, was neither leader nor individual, was but one sweated boy among many, doing machinelike work, leaving his personal mark on nothing; and it is not hard to imagine this as the beginning of his lifelong feeling that more than one institution can become a prison, and that imprisonment, in the sense of being shut off from others, can occur in many ways and under many circumstances. This feeling returns in several of his novels, culminating in *A Tale of Two Cities,* where, as we shall see, almost everybody is in some kind of prison.

A new world opened to Dickens after this dark early period, which now seemed forever lost in the past. His spirits bounded forward as he embraced his new prospects one after another. On finishing school, he first became a clerk in a law firm, then a newspaper reporter, then a parliamentary correspondent, having brought his shorthand to a peak of skill which surpassed that of all his older rivals. As if all this were not sufficiently taxing he began to write, in his leisure time, little vignettes, character studies, observations of London eccentrics, which he shortly published under the title *Sketches by Boz* (his brother's childhood mispronunciation of Moses, a family nickname). They brought him immediate success and the promise of an income.

On the strength of this achievement he married, and in one great year (1836–37) seemed to be started toward a brilliant literary career and a happy, fulfilling domestic life. But though the literary career did indeed become brilliant, the domestic life was marred and threatened from the start. It was, to begin with, partly the result of rebound. A four-year courtship of a pretty, empty-headed, frustrating coquette had left him with memories both bitter and passionate. Maria Beadnell, model for Dora the child-bride who dies young in *David Copperfield,* had in a sense also died young to Dickens, not only because she married another but because she was never fully alive to him, even during their courtship: she was a kind of porcelain doll, either untouchable or cold when touched. Whether in spite of this quality or because of it, Dickens remembered her with a romantic longing that is hard for us, over a century later, to give its proper credit.[4] Even twenty years after his marriage, when he heard from her again, all the old yearnings were reawakened. It was as if distance (and in this case time) lent the true enchantment to his ideal of femininity. He was to say of himself, partly in jest: "I don't like . . . Realities except when they are unattainable," and this seems to have been particularly true in his relations with women.[5] The reality he did attain with his wife Catherine Hogarth was a disappointment and frustration almost from the start. Their marriage eventually culminated in a crisis and then collapsed during the year preceding his work on *A Tale of Two Cities.*

With the advantages of hindsight, we can see a further way in which his marriage was marred and threatened, or at least oddly insecure; and this too is owing to his curious capacity for attachment to the unattainable, as well as his early and profound sense of "bereavement," of youth wasted and "thrown away." With the young couple when they moved into their first home had gone, for reasons which we do not know, Catherine's sister Mary Hogarth, beautiful, virtuous, intelligent, and gay, who within a year died very suddenly at the age of seventeen.[6] It was to Dickens an event at once fantastic and frighteningly real; and his reaction was extraordinary. "So perfect a creature never breathed. . . . She had not a fault. . . ." Laid to rest, she was "a silent but solemn witness that all health and beauty are but things of the hour. . . ." Finally, and strangely: "Thank God she died in my arms, and the very last words she whispered were of me. . . ." He took a ring from her finger and put it on his own, and never removed it; years later he was hoping to be buried next to her.

    [4] He tells Forster that the intensity of his nature is "desperate"; that he had seen Maria, when they were young, in a unique light; that no one could imagine "in the most distant degree" the pain of recollecting her in *David Copperfield*; and finally that to see or hear her now is to wander away "over the ashes of all that youth and hope in the wildest manner." John Forster, *The Life of Charles Dickens,* ed. J. W. T. Ley (New York: Doubleday Doran, 1928), p. 49.
    [5] Huntington Library MS, Dickens to Mrs. Watson, December 7, 1857. Quoted in Johnson, II, 911.
    [6] The known facts are related in Johnson, III, ii.

We are told that sentimentalizing of children and idealizing of women are Dickens traits: but his experiences and reactions suggest something deeper. V. S. Pritchett has said of Dickens's characters that they are distinguished by their solitariness—"they do not talk to one another; they talk to themselves"—and counters the view of E. M. Forster that they are external caricatures ("flat" in Forster's famous designation) by his own view that their posturing, their soliloquies, their eccentricities reveal "fragments of inner life." [7] Elsewhere Mr. Pritchett refers to the "weary pieties of realism that lie between us and a comprehension of Dickens." [8] If we couple such acute observations as these with our own analysis of the man at the crises of his life (including one more, the greatest, which we have yet to see), we discover in *A Tale of Two Cities* a writer who is struggling to present a kind of psychic overlay of fantasy on reality, a ghostly yet real heightening of experience, and a symbolic residue within even his most realistic characters. We become conscious of determining contrasts of light and shade in an innocent sunrise as Mr. Lorry looks out over a ploughed field after the fogs and ruts of the Dover road, or in a blood-red sunset on the stony face of the Marquis; we sense a Revolution that is as much an encroaching weave of footfalls and whispers as an historical fact; we see characters whose identity is more than half-symbolic and whose relationships are allegorical made secure nonetheless, through sheer circumstantiality and fine particulars, within a credible world of everyday experience—as when Sidney Carton, the great emblem of the outsider, quips in contemporary slang and drinks brandy with the spy Barsad. Dickens's feelings run deeper than we think, and his struggles often take him beyond the literary terms and conditions of his period: he manages a realistic tale of adventure that is at the same time fantastic, almost dreamlike, in its imaginative sway over the reader.

It is not only from women and children that Dickens often seems detached, though these as representatives of innocence and gentleness in a brutal world are always symbolically expressive.[9] He has a certain detachment from all his characters, placing them on high as it were; and, as Mr. Pritchett has noted, detaching them from each other as well as from himself. At the same time, no writer ever noted

---

[7] "Edwin Drood," in *The Living Novel and Later Appreciations* (New York: Random House, Inc., 1964), p. 86. Forster's opinions are in *Aspects of the Novel* (New York: Harcourt, Brace, 1927), pp. 67ff.

[8] "The Shocking Surgeon," in *The Living Novel,* p. 20. This is an essay on Smollett, whose work was a chief influence on Dickens.

[9] The pressure of his obsession with the death of young innocence may be reflected in what, in his description of Charles and Lucie's early years of marriage, seems all but forced: the loss of their young son (II, xxi, "Echoing Footsteps"); but the event is partly redeemed, and partly made symbolical, by the child's connection with Sidney Carton, whom he remembers at almost the last moment of his life, and who is himself like a dying child, being forlorn and separated from all others.

detail so masterfully; and, because he also seems to note it impersonally and inadvertently, the effect is to lend a kind of dramatic tension to the total "feel" of his work. Nowhere was this ever more true than in *A Tale of Two Cities,* as we have earlier suggested, where the author becomes refined almost wholly out of existence, the story itself "expressing" the characters, as he says.[10]

Dickens's life in these early years, indeed his whole public life, seems to belie assertions of his detachment, much more of his isolation or estrangement, just as his novels, so full of his stage-manager presence, seem to belie assertions of the author's absence. Yet *A Tale of Two Cities,* coming as we have said at a time of crisis in his life and innovative by intention, unmistakably gives us the perspectives af alienation; for his life did have a private, not to say a secret, side. True, no writer ever had greater success, ever lived a more ebullient, hard-driving, energetic, and gregarious public life. From *Boz* to *Pickwick* to *Oliver Twist* his creativity not only climbed but rather soared, in a way exploded. He became an editor of various periodicals, attending personally to every detail, as accomplished in business as in letters. He made an enormous number of friends, literary and nonliterary alike. He was much invited as an after-dinner speaker. He engaged in amateur theatricals and, again at about the time of *A Tale of Two Cities,* launched a new and consuming career as a public reader of his own works, in which he excelled as much as he had in authorship. He made two trips to America, where he lectured on the need for an international copyright law and gave public readings for which long lines of spectators patiently waited for hours; and he visited France and Italy and took a walking tour of England with this friend Wilkie Collins. Through all this his presence was always larger than life, always dramatic, always charged with an energy that remained inexhaustible. After one of his incomparably busy days he would often walk about London half the night, and he told Forster once that scaling all the Alps in Italy would not assuage his restlessness. Yet clearly this energy, hence this activity, was in part compulsive and hysterical, a sign of run-

[10] Some touches in the story which give a combined sense of nearness and detachment may be worth citing: one is the use made of the ploughed field mentioned above, a reminder of homely, workaday life, followed by Mr. Lorry's exclamation: "Gracious Creator of day! To be buried alive [which is one theme of the book, and one of Dickens's earlier titles for it] for eighteen years!"; another is the Negro cupids which so extraneously intrude upon Mr. Lorry's first interview with Lucie Manette; or there are the flies and the mirror, studiously observed by Dickens in the first courtroom; or the revealing marks on the Marquis's nose, more effective than a burst of rage; or the "shadow attendant on Madame Defarge" which falls on Lucie and her child. This same "shadow" is also a kind of disembodied romantic revolutionary, an abstraction like Delacroix's *Liberty Guiding the People,* another kind or level of reality, until reduced to still a third, that of mere uppity hussy by the blunt Englishness of Miss Pross: "Well, I am sure, Boldface! I hope *you* are pretty well!"

ning from or to something, trying to fill some gap that would not be filled. Though we may be surprised when we first encounter Santayana's remark: "He was a waif himself, and utterly disinherited," [11] if we remember those early crises, which he himself describes in terms so extreme that they make us think of an eternity and infinity of lostness—we have to acknowledge that so it was. And we understand better why, again surprisingly, he one day turns to his friend Forster with a sudden confession of his loneliness, and specifically of his great longing for "one friend and companion I never made, one happiness I missed in life." [12] He was indeed two realities: the unbelievably successful man of the world, but likewise the outsider: Oliver or Jo the crossing-sweeper or Sidney Carton, always either below or above the normal requirements and standards of civilization, never a part of it.

In 1857, when he was forty-two, when three-quarters of his work was done, he suddenly had reason to feel that the friend and companion had been found and the missed happiness lay in sight. But the experiences of that and the next year, though a certain personal fulfillment came of them, also resurrected in odd fashion the feelings that had been planted and augmented by his childhood losses and the death of Mary Hogarth. For years now, his marriage had been deteriorating, and his nervousness and restlessness with the harmless Catherine had correspondingly mounted. By ironic coincidence he had become attached once more to a sister-in-law, Georgina, as untouchable, and nearly as perfect, as Mary. He invokes her with something of the tone of twenty years before when he calls her indispensable, "the active spirit of the house." [13] Then overnight came a startling change: he met Ellen Ternan, an eighteen-year-old actress. His subsequent behavior was scarcely to his credit, but it indicates more than words how obsessed he was. He who had so long suffered from separateness now imposed a walling-off on his wife Catherine, and inevitably on himself. He ordered the passage between his room and hers to be closed by a wooden door, and (surely an elaboration of cruelty and doubly symbolic) the recess to be filled up with shelves. By June of 1858 Catherine had left his London house; Ellen was set up in a separate establishment; and in the following year the London house itself was given up and Dickens had gone to live in the house of his boyhood dreams at Gad's Hill near Rochester. He lived on there for another twelve years, writing *Great Expectations* and other works including the unfinished *Mystery of Edwin Drood*, and apparently remained the old gregarious Dickens who kept a permanently open door for his friends. But he was increasingly occupied with his public readings, and increasingly performed them under a

[11] "Dickens," in *Soliloquies in England* (London, 1922), p. 59.
[12] Letter to Forster [January, 1855], in *Letters*, II, 621.
[13] Letter to M. De la Rue, October 23, 1857, Berg MS, Dickens to De la Rue. Quoted in Johnson, II, 909 and n.

strain, a kind of frenzy and self-destructiveness that alarmed his doctor and his family until their combined pressure forced him to give them up, only three months before his death in June of 1870. He had never during these years been in touch with Catherine, and Ellen was at Gad's Hill when he died. He had presumably attained the unattainable: but the evidence suggests that not Ellen, but something deeper, farther away, more lost and mysterious, was his goal, and that he remained as unfulfilled and obsessed with his loneliness as ever.[14]

II

It was in the midst of this last great personal struggle that he began *A Tale of Two Cities*. He had long wanted to combine his bent toward social criticism and warning with the technique and point of view of the historical novel; and, further, he needed to find an escape from the torments of his struggle that would be at the same time a way of expressing it. Thus he would retain the experience, but he would remove it to a distance, an aesthetic distance. Only once before, in 1841 with *Barnaby Rudge*, had he attempted a historical novel; and the special difficulties and partial failure of that undertaking (an unaccustomed experience for him) had perhaps steered him back to contemporary scenes. But in 1857 and 1858, everything suddenly seemed transformed, and so he tried again, with various special helps he had not had before. One problem had been to combine the breadth of historical panorama with the particular, even eccentric or grotesque, observation that was his stock-in-trade. Another was to combine the truth of history with the "truth"—psychological, moral, dramatic—

---

[14] The best study of Dickens's relationship with Ellen Ternan is Ada Nisbet's *Dickens and Ellen Ternan* (Berkeley: University of California Press, 1952).

On Dickens's dramatic gesture of rejection, Professor Johnson comments that "the closing of that door after twenty-one years of married life was, in the tragedy of Dickens, symbolically as significant as Nora's slamming of the door in *A Doll's House*." Symbolically, and ironically: the effect on Dickens was only a parody of freedom. He was the more a prisoner: of a society not framed to accommodate his separation and the illicit arrangement with Ellen (a further discreditable and revealing act was his printing of a public explanation); of his own emotions and passions, not to be quelled by any external events; perhaps most cruelly of disappointment, since the remark, "I don't like Realities except when they are unattainable," probably reflects the deepest truth of his mental life and of his creative force. Professor Johnson adds, on the subject of his hysterical pursuit of exhausting public readings: "Perhaps Dickens would have felt shocked had he been accused of a deliberate effort at suicide. . . . But he had ceased to care what happened. All his fame had not brought him the things he most deeply wanted." He also suggests that the enchantment Dickens had felt in Maria had never been there, but had been imposed all along by "the radiant hallucination of youth" (Johnson, II, 911 and n., 1104; II, 835). We shall see later a different use of the idea of "hallucination" to explain Dickens's peculiar vision of life as it appears in his novels.

of literary expression. Still another was to imagine characters who would have a both public and private, historical and personal interest and to house them in a story that itself had this double kind of relevance. And finally, there was always in Dickens's case, especially in his impending crisis, the need to weave in and make relevant special themes and interests out of his most personal, intimate, psychological history. To reach all these objectives in a single, unified work was doubtless impossible, even for a genius of Dickens's surpassing powers. But if we know something of the many motives and materials he was working with, we shall better understand both the successes and the partial failures of the *Tale*.

The reality-fantasy "mix" runs through all Dickens's work.[15] In the *Tale*, the plot seems to bring us merely a straightforward story of adventure, danger, and suspense, with a certain amount of commentary, characterization, and atmosphere added. But without violating "reality," Dickens has managed to give everything—including the plot—a coloring of fantasy. The basic "detail"—the basic fact—of the whole enterprise is the Revolution itself. But it is the effect of the Revolution, its immediate and shocking effect, on individuals that suits Dickens's metamorphosizing imagination best, hence its horrific and terrific aspects, its nightmare side in the Terror and in its prelude, the September, 1792, Massacre. His treatment of historical event in *Barnaby Rudge* shows the same tendencies. On the one hand, he is interested in a moment of history—the anti-Catholic riots inspired by the half-mad Lord Gordon in the late eighteenth century. On the other, it is its

[15] Although *A Tale of Two Cities* does not, in its economy, show as often as some of his novels his tendency to give life and feeling to inanimate objects, it does produce a dream-like effect at important points—the forays of the mob, the burning of the chateau, the Carmagnole, the counting of heads—which illustrates the blend. Dickens's strong sense of a kind of hallucinatory participation in the works of his fancy was, as it happens, noted in his time, but not always with critical approval (see Forster's comments, pp. 716ff, on a review of Dickens's work at large published after Dicken's death by George Henry Lewes). Of the idea of this work, chiefly no doubt of the sacrifice of Sidney Carton, he says in his preface, ". . . it has had complete possession of me; I have so far verified what is done and suffered in these pages, as that I have certainly done and suffered it all myself."

For further comment on this subject, with illustrations from other novels of Dickens's, see Dorothy van Ghent, "The Dickens World: A View from Todgers's," originally published in the *Sewanee Review*, LVIII (1950), 419–38; and John Bayley, "*Oliver Twist:* 'Things as They Really Are'," originally published in *Dickens and the Twentieth Century*, ed. John Gross and Gabriel Pearson (London: Routledge & Kegan Paul, Ltd., 1962; Toronto: University of Toronto Press, 1962), both reprinted in the *Twentieth Century Views* volume *Dickens: A Collection of Critical Essays*, ed. Martin Price (Prentice-Hall, Inc., 1967), pp. 24–38 and 83–96 respectively. For the form which this feature of Dickens's mind takes in *A Tale of Two Cities*, see the selections in this volume from Professor Taylor Stoehr's *Dickens: The Dreamer's Stance* (Ithaca: Cornell University Press, 1965).

bloodiness, violence, and insanity that attracts him, countering the rationalism and rigor that Victorian society in general, and his own personal life in particular, so full of demands and obligations, thrust upon him.[16] Outward fact and psychic impulse here probably served each other.[17]

Madness is thematic also in the *Tale*. Dr. Manette is mad, or so disoriented as to be mad in effect, when his daughter Lucie is first led to him. He is mad from his senseless imprisonment of eighteen years— or, worse than senseless, the imprisonment to which he is condemned as the result of an accidental discovery made while performing a virtuous act. After he is rescued, he is brought back to health through love and care. But then the pressure of outside events—the fear of having to enact the whole nightmare over again, either in his own person or in that of others he loves—forces his madness to return. And this time it is a true madness: a doubling of the original condition, a sense that one is never to be free. Doubling in this sense, and in many senses, plays a role in the significant structure of the book. It is not of course the same thing as madness: but it is related in the sense that

[16] Mr. Pritchett, referring to Edmund Wilson's earlier comment on this quality in Dickens, mentions "the twin strains of rebel and criminal in his nature." ("Edwin Drood," in *Living Appreciations*, p. 87). And Forster tells of how he talked Dickens out of his original intention of having the riots led by actual maniacs. But Dickens makes much of *comparing* the actions of the mob to those of maniacs, thus keeping part of the point: he describes how one dabbles in fire as if it were water, how another melts his own head under a stream of molten lead, etc. George Orwell says of these events that "Dickens . . . delights in describing scenes in which the 'dregs' of the population behave with atrocious bestiality. These chapters are of great psychological interest, because they show how deeply he had brooded on this subject. The things he describes can only have come out of his imagination, for no riots on anything like the same scale had happened in his lifetime" (Forster, p. 168; Orwell, "Charles Dickens," in *Dickens, Dali and Others* [New York: Reynal and Hitchcock, 1946], pp. 11–12).

[17] A hideous and curious example—curious in that Dickens both included it and yet had to be so reticent that it hardly makes sense as it stands—and a kind of epitome of the reality-fantasy-nightmare identity is an instance of historical allusion apparently put in for those who had read Carlyle's *French Revolution*. It is the farthest reach of shocking affront offered to Marie Antoinette, when one of the murderers of the Princesse de Lamballe fashions a mustache of pubic hair and flaunts it under the Queen's window. Carlyle's comment is Dickensian in its joining of horror with grandeur of feeling, and was perhaps meant by Dickens to be part of the specific allusion: "She was beautiful, she was good, she had known no happiness. Young hearts, generation after generation, will think with themselves: O worthy of worship, thou king-descended, god-descended, and poor sister-woman! why was not I there . . . ?" (*French Revolution*, III, i, 4). Dickens says only, and as it stands perplexingly: "False eyebrows and false moustaches were stuck upon them, and their hideous countenances were all bloody and sweaty, and all awry with howling, and all staring and glaring with beastly excitement and lack of sleep." Which of course, even without the specific allusion, makes for something of the effect of fantasy becoming real.

when anything is doubled, neither half can be said to make up the whole reality so that each alone is incomplete, a deficiency or distortion: though both together, in a specific situation, may only mean a reinforcement of nightmare. Thus Charles Darnay's double arrest, thus the sudden casting of Dr. Manette in the role of accuser, an especially apt irony since he had earlier been cast in the role of injured innocence. These have been criticized as forced or rigged: but equally they can stand, symbolically, as instances of the contradictory nature of subjective experience, even of the self, in relation to events. Certainly Dr. Manette had as much reason, or more, to curse the house of Evrémonde, as to honor and protect his son-in-law; and one basic lesson of the Revolution was that as it gathered strength it turned on itself. This at least seems to have been Dickens's feeling.

Doubling of one kind and another, whether as indication of madness or simply as a prime technique of symbolism in the fantasizing of reality, recurs throughout the book. The most obvious example is the physical resemblance of Charles Darnay and Sidney Carton— which looks on the surface like a trick, a plot device that hurts both theme and characterization. Yet if we move away from the realistic and literalistic, we can see this form of doubling as a representation of two worlds, the social or collective on the one hand, the individual or subjective—or, in Freud's terminology, "instinctual"—on the other. This second cannot live with the first; its way is the way of the outsider, the creature of waste places: but at moments of crisis it can save the first. Charles Darnay, the admirer of George Washington, is the "new man" of his time, unable to speak with his immovable uncle, the representative of the old regime, a gargoyle whom only the fire of revolution can melt or move; but in a way he is as immovable as his uncle, immovably virtuous and democratic, socially conscious. Sidney Carton, his counterpart, the outsider, is on the contrary moved from extreme to extreme: from an emptiness, desolation, and uncaring that place him below the norm of the collective, to a willed love and sacrifice that lift him above it. He is always isolated: but his isolation at first rejects society, at last embraces it, as when he says, "I see a beautiful city and a brilliant people rising from this abyss. . . ."

One of the best touches of counterrealism in the book is Dickens's refusal to account for Sidney Carton's isolation and emptiness; he is, at first, a jackal lurking out of nowhere. With Madame Defarge, perhaps wrongly, Dickens attempts a compromise, one of the indications of his struggle to bring together disparate materials. She too is a lonely stalking animal, a deadly counterpart of Lucie Manette, the two of them representing opposite versions of the forever untouchable woman in Dickens's longing imagination. At first, she is unmotivated, a creature of pure malignancy like Claggart in Melville's *Billy Budd,* or like

Iago: a cold monomaniac whose whole identity lies in hate and the meditation of revenge.[18] To be sure, the general oppression of the regime forms a general motivation; but she towers above the general world by virtue of her inflexible obsession, inhabiting a world of her own as much as the Marquis, a self-defining world. Surprisingly, toward the end, Dickens yields to realism and gives her a specific and credible motivation. This is jarring. At this point, both the Marquis and Sidney Carton, the one with a generalized motivation, the other with none at all, come off better. Yet she remains an instructive instance of Dickens's attempt throughout this novel to identify fantasy with reality —as in his own life at this momentous crisis he was likewise attempting to do.

Prison and imprisonment also color this novel and remove our thoughts from motivation. More perhaps than any other work by Dickens—though there are prisons and imprisonment in plenty elsewhere —this one is about people trapped in some kind of vise, consequently shut away from others, or susceptible of shutting others away. The Marquis is pent up by the logic of his world—only death can reach him. So, at an opposite pole, is Madame Defarge. Dr. Manette returns compulsively to shoemaking at a moment of crisis, the prisoner of past suffering and solitude; and he finds later in the story that his accusations as a prisoner return to thwart his new and larger acceptance of life. Lucie Manette's imprisonment is in passive purity, always likely to be crushed between mighty opposites; and Charles Darnay, courageous but helpless, is rendered a prisoner by his own probity. In a way the whole outlook is pessimistic, individual frailty pitted against public insanity, with salvation coming only accidentally and at the cost of yet another life. Even Sidney Carton's self-sacrifice has been depressed in value by some critics, who offer the opinion that when he gave up his life he gave up only what had been adjudged by the author and himself to be nearly worthless.

On the negative side, such considerations suggest that the novel discloses Dickens's despair at the choices before him: imprisonment, or, as the price of breaking out, madness and death. More positively, it reveals his ability to give his personal concerns an artistic shape. Despite its shortcomings, the work's effect is finally powerful and centralized. It escapes from the pull of excessive detail and plotting to a level of symbolic action as entrenched power, destructive revenge, thwarted love, isolation, and reconciliation play out their drama. And it is Dickens's closest approximation to the effect of tragedy. The significance of Sidney Carton's life is his growth to a new awareness and new love, a love perhaps higher than Dickens himself could

---

[18] Orwell says of her that she is "certainly Dickens's most successful attempt at a *malignant* character" ("Charles Dickens," p. 15).

achieve but one that he could—and it is all we ask of a writer—vividly imagine and record. Hence, in one way, this is Dickens's most personal novel, where he purged himself of one part, at least, of his distress; while in another way, it is his most impersonal, the grand objectivity of the historical events it springs from, the steady movement of its action, and the economy and integrity of its details keeping him at a workmanlike distance from his materials, and enabling him to achieve a purer effect at the close than he had ever achieved before.

III

This very purity caused concern when the novel first appeared. The author's friend and great admirer, John Forster, became altogether apologetic when, after Dickens's death, he analyzed it in his biography:

> . . . there is no instance in his novels, excepting this, of a deliberate and planned departure from the method of treatment which had been preeminently the source of his popularity as a novelist. To rely less upon character than upon incident, and to resolve that his actors should be expressed by the story more than they should express themselves by dialogue, was for him a hazardous, and can hardly be called an entirely successful, experiment.[19]

Then, as if to save the book from his own faint praise, he turns to its nobility at the end: "Dickens speaks of his design to make impressive the dignity of Carton's death, and in this he succeeded perhaps even beyond his expectation." [20] Forster thus takes the high road of moral feeling in judging the book and quotes enthusiastically the American critic, Grant White, for his lavish praise of Sidney Carton's last moments. The grandeur of this episode, along with the uncluttered theatricality of the main characters and the main action, formed for many years the chief points of emphasis for critics of the novel and its chief ground of popularity with the public.[21]

Some contemporary and later opinion remained adverse. A severe attack appeared in the *Saturday Review*, a Tory journal hostile to many reformist ideas, by Sir James Fitzjames Stephen, an attorney and judge who had been angered by Dickens's satirical treatment of legal and court procedures in *Bleak House*. It is an early example of wrongheadedness in criticism of this novel, yet occasionally shrewd enough

---

[19] Forster, p. 731.
[20] *Ibid.*
[21] A play of the time, *The Dead Heart*, by Watts Phillips, is an early reflection of the dramatic values of *A Tale of Two Cities*, as is Freeman Wills's play, *The Only Way* (1890), popular in both England and America; not to mention the MGM movie classic of the 30s, or the recent report that still another film version is to be made in the 70s.

to provoke an answer.[22] It was shortly answered [23] by a review in the periodical *The Press,* which made the point that the French Revolution is, to the greater effectiveness of "the storyteller's art," not allowed to intermingle in the action save as a *Deus ex machina;* that though the book runs the risk of morbidity in its first descriptions of Dr. Manette's insanity, it is saved by "the admirable account" to which his character is turned in the denouement; that Sidney Carton, "whether or not we admit that so peculiar a compound of opposites be humanly possible," represents the highest "poetical" reach of Dickens's genius; and that the book's few faults are chiefly faults of style: his "inveterate formalism," and (oddly harsh phrase) the "malicious affectation aforethought in which he wilfully and perversely insists upon dressing his best and his worst thoughts alike, as in the stiffest Prussian uniform." ("It was the best of times, it was the worst of times. . . .") But neither this piece nor Stephen's finds a level sufficiently above the work to see the whole, or sufficiently near it to see the contribution of the details. This effort was left to modern criticism.

Though Dickens hoped it was his best story, many moderns and near-moderns have named it his worst.[24] George Saintsbury, George Gissing, and Arnold Bennett found it unimpressive, an anomaly among Dickens's work, though Gissing had the perception to see that Dickens had produced "something like a true tragedy." [25] Another disappointed group was made up of those who preferred the Dickens of *Pickwick*; still another, of those who found the presentation of French culture and manners distorted or defective; and yet a third, of those who questioned Dickens's optimism in his portrayal of a beautiful city with a brilliant people and a Rousseauistic peasantry. There has also, more pertinently, been complaint about the mixture of realism with contrivances of suspense, coincidence, and sensationalism. Here Dickens himself had some opinions worth noting. He liked to observe that life is full of odd ties of circumstance and fortune, and of the *Tale* he says specifically:

[22] It contains such phrases as: "The broken-backed way in which the story maunders along. . . ." "The whole art is to take a melancholy subject, and rub the reader's nose in it . . ." and ". . . this is the very lowest of low styles of art." The whole review has been reprinted in *The Dickens Critics,* ed. George H. Ford and Lauriat Lane, Jr. (Ithaca: Cornell University Press, 1961), pp. 38–46.

[23] Without mention of the *Saturday Review* or of Stephen; but John Blackwood writes to George Eliot on December 25, 1859: "Look at the Press this week and you will see our friends of the Saturday Review as pleasantly flayed as you could wish for their insolent attack upon Dickens" (*The George Eliot Letters,* ed. Gordon Haight [New Haven: Yale University Press, 1954], III, 237).

[24] The chief source of the following summarized information is a very thorough and documented survey by Professor Heinz Reinhold, "Charles Dickens Roman *A Tale of Two Cities* und das Publikum," *Germanisch-romanische Monatsschrift,* XXXVI (1955), 319–37.

[25] *Charles Dickens: A Critical Study* (London, 1904), p. 67.

I am not clear . . . respecting that canon of fiction which forbids the interposition of accident in such a case as Madame Defarge's death. Where the accident is inseparable from the passion and emotion of the character; where it is strictly consistent with the whole design, and arises out of some culminating proceeding on the part of the character which the whole story has led up to; it seems to become . . . an act of divine justice. And when I use Miss Pross . . . to bring about that catastrophe, I have the positive intention of making that half-comic intervention a part of the desperate woman's failure; and of opposing that mean death, instead of a desperate one in the streets, which she wouldn't have minded, to the dignity of Carton's. Wrong or right, this was all design. . . .[26]

This may not justify Dickens's use of coincidence to the taste of every reader: but it shows that he held it to be more than mere contrivance, either because it was in fact realistic or had thematic relevances beyond the claims of realism.

A final point of attack has always been the high romanticism of Carton's sacrificial death, which is seen as an outcropping of Dickens's insensitivity to psychological nuance. Placed beside George Eliot and Flaubert, he can indeed be made to look a caricaturist. But there are other perspectives on his work which show us, through all his apparent flatness and simplicity, a "vision" unique in fiction, one in which the caricatures, the plot tricks, and the large, blunt emotions lock in, as behind a series of floodgates, a vast expanse of mythic contemplation involving mysterious figures (Sidney Carton, Madame Defarge), fateful journeys (the Marquis to his death, Darnay to his survival, Carton to his salvation), and a world in flames or darkness, yearning for the light. Modern criticism is trying to provide the appropriate keys for these locks, keys that will fit.

The essays and parts of essays reprinted here represent a body of modern criticism that shows the wide range of approaches possible in interpreting *A Tale of Two Cities.* Generally, they fall into three groups: (1) those that consider the work mainly as an expression of Dickens's personal obsessions and torments during the years just before its composition; (2) those that deal with its sources, of which there is a surprising variety, ranging from sensational literature to Bulwer Lytton's novel *Zanoni,* itself a handling of the theme of spiritual regeneration during the French Revolution but with mystical and magical overtones such as Dickens eschews; and (3) those that attempt a definitive assessment by examining the elements of the work itself. Earle Davis and Jack Lindsay discuss circumstances and sources, the first concentrating on literary and editorial matters, the second on the relevance of Dickens's personal life to his workmanship. The late

[26] Letter to Forster [August, 1859], in *Letters,* III, 117.

William H. Marshall takes up the neglected topic of symbolism and
rhetoric, tracing patterns of image structure, a theme on which John
Gross comments more broadly, assessing image-idea relationships and
their expressive function. Such approaches are continued at greater
length and with greater specialization by Taylor Stoehr, who argues
persuasively that the structure of the novel is dreamlike in its pattern
of association, its use of metonymy, and its grand pervasive metaphors.
G. Robert Stange differentiates the actual *Tale* from the "tale" cat-
egory by showing that it has a wholeness rich in detail, image, and
thematic implication. Among the *View Points*, Bernard Shaw's
provocative comment tries to make us believe in a vulgarized Dickens,
an entertainer without a moral core; George Orwell, taking pre-
dictably a political-historical approach, nevertheless makes acute and
surprising observations on Dickens's eye for detail and his ability to
evolve an atmosphere—sinister, haunting, unforgettable; Sergei Eisenstein writes excitingly of the "overlay" or "montage" effect in Dickens, with examples chiefly from *Oliver Twist*, yet suggestively touching
on the *Tale*; A. O. J. Cockshut strikes a Shakespearean note in survey-
ing the whole achievement: ". . . in the end . . . the vivid journalist,
the entertainer, and the artist are triumphantly at one"; and Taylor
Stoehr, in a second excerpt, extends his treatment of Dickens's special
powers of organization, particularly the power of giving life to objects,
and of conjoining realism and metaphor to produce the effect of myth.

PART ONE

Interpretations

A Tale of Two Cities

by John Gross

A Tale of Two Cities ends fairly cheerfully with its hero getting killed; Dickens's previous novel, *Little Dorrit*, ends in deep gloom with its hero getting married. Violence offers Dickens a partial release from the sense of frustration and despondency which crept over him during the eighteen-fifties; the shadow of the Marshalsea lifts a little with the storming of the Bastille, and everyone remembers *A Tale of Two Cities* above all for the intoxication of its crowd-scenes. In fact they take up less space than one supposes in retrospect, and for the most part the atmosphere is every bit as stifling as that of *Little Dorrit*. Dickens originally thought of calling the book *Buried Alive*, and at its heart lie images of death and, much less certainly, of resurrection: themes which foreshadow *Our Mutual Friend*.

The story opens with the feeblest of resurrections, the recall to life of Doctor Manette. His daughter is afraid that she is going to meet his ghost, a fear that is almost justified when she actually sees his spectral face and hears his voice, so faint and lacking in life and resonance that it is "like the last feeble echo of a sound made long and long ago . . . like a voice underground." (Bk. I, Ch. 6.) The whole novel is thronged with ghosts; from the mist moving forlornly up the Dover Road "like an evil spirit seeking rest and finding none" to the gunsmoke which as it clears suggests Madame Defarge's soul leaving her body, there are scores of references to spectres, phantoms, and apparitions. The penniless émigrés haunt Tellson's like familiar spirits; Lorry sees the likeness of the Lucie whom he once knew pass like a breath across the pier-glass behind her; the fountains of the château show ghostly in the dawn—but it would be tedious to compile a catalogue.

Reprinted, with permission, from Dickens and the Twentieth Century, *ed. John Gross and Gabriel Pearson (Toronto: University of Toronto Press; London: Routledge & Kegan Paul, Ltd., 1962), pp. 187–97. Copyright © University of Toronto Press and Routledge & Kegan Paul, Ltd.*

Such ghostliness suggests, first of all, a sense of unreality, of the death in life to which men are reduced by imprisonment, psychological or actual. To Darnay, the prisoners in La Force, going through the motions of elegance and pride in the midst of squalor, are ghosts all, "waiting their dismissal from the desolate shore," and the scene simply "the crowning unreality of his long unreal ride." (Bk. III, Ch. 1.) But ghosts are also the creatures of false or, at any rate, imperfect resurrection: the grave gives up its dead reluctantly, and the prisoner who has been released is still far from being a free man. The inmates of the Bastille, suddenly given their liberty by "the storm that had burst their tomb," are anything but overjoyed: "all scared, all lost, all wondering and amazed, as if the Last Day were come, and those who rejoiced around them were all lost spirits." (Bk. II, Ch. 21.) Even the phlegmatic Darnay, after his Old Bailey acquittal, "scarcely seems to belong to this world again." As for Doctor Manette, he has been as deeply scarred by his prison experience as William Dorrit. Lucie's love is not enough in itself to stop him from retreating into his shoe-making, and it takes a symbolic act of violence to complete the cure; he is fully restored to himself only after Mr. Lorry has hacked to pieces his cobbler's bench, "while Miss Pross held the candle as if she were assisting at a murder." (Book II, Ch. 19). But by this time the centre of interest in the book has shifted unmistakably to Sydney Carton.

The prison and the grave are linked in Dickens's mind with the idea that "every human creature is constituted to be that profound secret and mystery to every other." We live in essential isolation; in each heart there is, "in some of its imaginings, a secret to the heart nearest it. Something of the awfulness, even of death itself, is referable to this . . . In any of the burial-places of this city through which I pass, is there a sleeper more inscrutable than its busy inhabitants are, in their innermost personality, to me, or than I am to them?" (Bk. I, Ch. 3.) On his journey to greet the newly released Manette, Mr. Lorry feels as if he is going to unearth a secret as well as dig up a dead man; in his dream the grave is confused with the underground strong-rooms at Tellson's, and he fancies himself digging "now with a spade, now with a great key, now with his hands." In his hotel room, the two tall candles are reflected on every leaf of the heavy dark tables, "as if *they* were buried in deep graves of dark mahogany, and no light to speak of could be expected of them until they were dug out." (Bk. I, Ch. 4.)

This oppressive sense of mystery generates suspicion and fear. "All secret men are soon terrified," Dickens tells us in connection with Barsad, the police spy; but we are in a world where everyone is a secret man, a world of whispers and echoes. On the Dover Mail "the guard suspected the passengers, the passengers suspected one another and the guard, they all suspected everybody else"; when Darnay returns to

France, "the universal watchfulness so encompassed him, that if he had been taken in a net, or were being forwarded to his destination in a cage, he could not have felt his freedom more completely gone." (Bk. III, Ch. 1.) Even in the haven established for Doctor Manette near Soho Square there is foreboding in the air, in the echoes which Lucie makes out to be "the echoes of all the footsteps that are coming by and by into our lives." An accurate enough premonition of the noise of feet and voices pouring into the Paris courtyard which first draws her attention to the bloodstained grindstone, or of the troubled movement and shouting round a street-corner which herald the Carmagnole. Carton's last impression, too, is to be of "the pressing on of many footsteps" on the outskirts of the crowd round the guillotine. Footsteps suggest other people, and in *A Tale of Two Cities* other people are primarily a threat and a source of danger. The little group around Doctor Manette is as self-contained as any in Dickens, but it enjoys only a precarious safety; the emblematic golden arm on the wall at Soho Square is always capable of dealing a poisoned blow.

A Tale of Two Cities is a tale of two heroes. The theme of the double has such obvious attractions for a writer preoccupied with disguises, rival impulses, and hidden affinities that it is surprising that Dickens didn't make more use of it elsewhere. But no one could claim that his handling of the device is very successful here, or that he has managed to range the significant forces of the novel behind Carton and Darnay. Darnay is, so to speak, the accredited representative of Dickens in the novel, the "normal" hero for whom a happy ending is still possible. It has been noted, interestingly enough, that he shares his creator's initials—and that is pretty well the only interesting thing about him. Otherwise he is a pasteboard character, completely undeveloped. His position as an exile, his struggles as a language-teacher, his admiration for George Washington are so many openings thrown away.

Carton, of course, is a far more striking figure. He belongs to the line of cultivated wastrels who play an increasingly large part in Dickens's novels during the second half of his career, culminating in Eugene Wrayburn; his clearest predecessor, as his name indicates, is the luckless Richard Carstone of *Bleak House*. He has squandered his gifts and drunk away his early promise; his will is broken, but his intellect is unimpaired. In a sense, his opposite is not Darnay at all, but the aggressive Stryver, who makes a fortune by picking his brains. Yet there is something hollow about his complete resignation to failure: his self-abasement in front of Lucie, for instance. ("I am like one who died young . . . I know very well that you can have no tenderness for me . . .") For, stagy a figure though he is, Carton does suggest what Thomas Hardy calls "fearful unfulfilments"; he still has vitality, and it is hard to believe that he has gone down without a struggle. The total effect is one of energy held unnaturally in check: the bottled-up frustration which Carton represents must spill over somewhere.

Carton's and Darnay's fates are entwined from their first meeting, at the Old Bailey trial. Over the dock there hangs a mirror: "crowds of the wicked and the wretched had been reflected in it, and had passed from its surface and this earth's together. Haunted in a most ghastly manner that abominable place would have been, if the glass could ever have rendered back its reflections, as the ocean is one day to give up its dead." (Bk. II, Ch. 2.) After Darnay's acquittal we leave him with Carton, "so like each other in feature, so unlike in manner, both reflected in the glass above them." Reflections, like ghosts, suggest unreality and self-division, and at the end of the same day Carton stares at his own image in the glass and upbraids it: "Why should you particularly like a man who resembles you? There is nothing in you to like: you know that. Ah, confound you! . . . Come on, and have it out in plain words! You hate the fellow." (Bk. II, Ch. 4.) In front of the mirror, Carton thinks of changing places with Darnay; at the end of the book, he is to take the other's death upon him. Dickens prepares the ground: when Darnay is in jail, it is Carton who strikes Mr. Lorry as having "the wasted air of a prisoner," and when he is visited by Carton on the rescue attempt, he thinks at first that he is "an apparition of his own imagining." But Dickens is determined to stick by Darnay: a happy ending *must* be possible. As Lorry and his party gallop to safety with the drugged Darnay, there is an abrupt switch to the first person: "The wind is rushing after us, and the clouds are flying after us, and the moon is plunging after us, and the whole wild night is in pursuit of us; but so far, we are pursued by nothing else." (Bk. III, Ch. 13.) *We* can make our escape, however narrowly; Carton, expelled from our system, must be abandoned to his fate.

But the last word is with Carton—the most famous last word in Dickens, in fact. Those who take a simplified view of Dickens's radicalism, or regard him as one of nature's Marxists, can hardly help regretting that *A Tale of Two Cities* should end as it does. They are bound to feel, with Edgar Johnson, that "instead of merging, the truth of revolution and the truth of sacrifice are made to appear in conflict." A highly personal, indeed a unique crisis cuts across public issues and muffles the political message. But this is both to sentimentalize Dickens's view of the revolution, and to miss the point about Carton. The cynical judgment that his sacrifice was trifling, since he had nothing to live for, is somewhat nearer the mark. Drained of the will to live, he is shown in the closing chapters of the book as a man courting death, and embracing it when it comes. "In seasons of pestilence, some of us will have a secret attraction to the disease—a terrible passing inclination to die of it. And all of us have like wonders hidden in our breasts, only needing circumstances to evoke them." (Bk. III, Ch. 6.) It is Carton rather than Darnay who is "drawn to the loadstone rock." [1] On his last walk around Paris, a passage which Shaw cites in the preface to *Man and Superman* as proof of Dickens's essentially irreligious nature, his thoughts run on religion: "I am the Resurrection and the Life." But his impressions are all of death: the day comes coldly, "looking like a dead face out of the sky," while on the river "a trading boat, with a sail of the softened colour of a dead leaf, then glided into his view, floated by him, and died away." (Bk. III, Ch. 9.) His walk recalls an earlier night, when he wandered round London with "wreaths of dust spinning round and round before the morning blast, as if the desert sand had risen far away and the first spray of it in its advance had begun to overwhelm the city." (Bk. II, Ch. 5.) Then, with the wilderness bringing home to him a sense of the wasted powers within him, he saw a momentary mirage of what he might have achieved and was reduced to tears; but now that the city has been overwhelmed in earnest, he is past thinking of what might have been. "It is a far, far better thing that I do, than I have ever done"—but the "better thing" might just as well be committing suicide as laying down his life for Darnay. At any rate, he thinks of himself as going towards rest, not towards resurrection.

By this time the revolution has become simply the agency of death, the storm that overwhelms the city. Or rather, all the pent-up fury and resentment that is allowed no outlet in the "personal" side of the book, with Carton kow-towing to Stryver and nobly renouncing Lucie, boils over in revolutionary violence: Dickens dances the Carmagnole, and howls for blood with the mob. Frightened by the forces which he has released, he views the revolution with hatred and disgust; he doesn't record a single incident in which it might be shown as beneficent, constructive or even tragic. Instead, it is described time and again in terms of pestilence and madness. Dickens will hear nothing of noble aspirations; the disorder of the whole period is embodied in the dervishes who dance the Carmagnole—"no fight could have been half so terrible." Confronted with the crowd, Dickens reaches

---

[1] Darnay, who only comes to life in the face of death, is nevertheless obsessed with the guillotine. He has "a strange besetting desire to know what to do when the time came, a desire gigantically disproportionate to the few swift moments to which it referred; a wondering that was more like the wondering of some other spirit within his, than his own." (Bk. III, Ch. 13.) Carton's spirit, perhaps; through the exigencies of the plot, Dickens has got the wires crossed.

for his gun; he looks into eyes "which any unbrutalized beholder would have given twenty years of life, to have petrified with a well-directed gun." (Bk. III, Ch. 2.) That "well-directed" has the true ring of outraged rate-paying respectability, while the image seems oddly out of place in a book which has laid so much stress on the stony faces and petrified hearts of the aristocracy.

Dickens can only deal with mob-violence in a deliberately pictur-esque story set in the past. But *A Tale of Two Cities,* written by a middle-aged man who could afford a longer perspective at a time when Chartism was already receding into history, is not quite analogous to *Barnaby Rudge.* There, however contemptible we are meant to find the world of Sir John Chester, the riots are an explosion of madness and nothing more. But the French Revolution compels Dickens to acquire a theory of history, however primitive: "crush humanity out of shape once more, under similar hammers, and it will twist itself into the same tortured forms." (Bk. III, Ch. 15.) The revolutionaries return evil for evil; the guillotine is the product not of innate depravity but of intolerable oppression. If Dickens's sympathies shift towards the aristocrats as soon as they become victims, he can also show a grim restraint; he underlines the horror of Foulon's death, strung up with a bunch of grass tied to his back (how his imagination pounces on such a detail!), but he never allows us to forget who Foulon was. Nor does he have any sympathy with those who talk of the Revolution "as though it were the only harvest under the skies that had never been sown," although he himself is at times plainly tempted to treat it as an inexplicable calamity, a rising of the sea (the gaoler at La Force has the bloated body of a drowned man, and so forth) or a rising of fire: the flames which destroy the château of St. Evrémonde "blow from the infernal regions," convulsing nature until the lead boils over inside the stone fountains. But cause and effect are never kept out of sight for long; Dickens is always reminding himself that the Revolution, though "a frightful moral disorder," was born of "unspeakable suffering, in-tolerable oppression, and heartless indifference." Society was diseased before the fever broke out: the shattered cask of wine which at the out-set falls on the "crippling" stones of Saint Antoine is scooped up in little mugs of "mutilated" earthenware.

But to grasp a patient's medical history is not to condone his dis-ease, and Dickens is unyielding in his hostility to the crowd. The buzzing of the flies on the scent for carrion at the Old Bailey trial and the mass-rejoicing at Roger Cly's funeral are early indications of what he feels. The courtroom in Paris is also full of buzzing and stirring, but by this time the atmosphere has become positively cannibalistic; a jury of dogs has been empanelled to try the deer, Madame Defarge "feasts" on the prisoner, Jacques III, with his very Carlylean croak, is described as an epicure.

Whatever Dickens's motives, a good deal of this is no doubt perfectly valid; morbid fantasies can still prompt shrewd observations, as when we are shown Darnay, the prisoner of half an hour, already learning to count the steps as he is led away to his cell. In particular, Dickens recognizes the ways in which a period of upheaval can obliterate the individual personality; there is no more telling detail in the book than the roll-call of the condemned containing the names of a prisoner who has died in jail and two who have already been guillotined, all of them forgotten. Insane suspicion, senseless massacres, the rise to power of the worst elements: in the era of Gladstonian budgets Dickens understands the workings of a police state.

But it would be ludicrous to claim very much for the accuracy of Dickens's account of the French Revolution as such. There are scarcely any references to the actual course of events, and no suggestion at all that the revolution had an intellectual or idealistic content, while the portrayal of fanaticism seems childish if we compare it even with something as one-sided as *The Gods are Athirst*. For the purposes of the novel, the revolution is the Defarges, and although Carton foresees that Defarge in his turn will perish on the guillotine, he has no inkling of how the whole internecine process will ever come to a halt. As for Madame Defarge, she is as much driven by fate as the stony-hearted Marquis, with his coachmen cracking their whips like the Furies: the time has laid "a dreadfully disfiguring hand upon her." Her last entry is her most dramatic. Miss Pross is bathing her eyes to rid herself of feverish apprehensions, when she suddenly appears—materializes, one might say—in the doorway:

> The basin fell to the ground broken, and the water flowed to the feet of Madame Defarge. By strange stern ways, and through much staining blood, those feet had come to meet that water. (Bk. III, Ch. 14.)

We are reminded, by rather too forcible a contrast, of the broken cask of red wine which prefaces Madame Defarge's first appearance in the novel. Her element, from the very start, is blood.

Still, *A Tale of Two Cities* is not a private nightmare, but a work which continues to give pleasure. Dickens's drives and conflicts are his raw material, not the source of his artistic power, and in itself the fact that the novel twists the French Revolution into a highly personal fantasy proves nothing: so, after all, does *The Scarlet Pimpernel*. Everything depends on the quality of the writing—which is usually one's cue, in talking about Dickens, to pay tribute to his exuberance and fertility. Dickens's genius inheres in minute particulars; later we may discern patterns of symbolism and imagery, a design which lies deeper than the plot, but first we are struck by the lavish heaping-up of acute observations, startling similes, descriptive flourishes, circumstantial embroidery. Or such is the case with every Dickens novel except for the *Tale,* which is written in a style so grey and unadorned that many readers are reluctant to grant it a place in the Canon at all. Dickens wouldn't be Dickens if there weren't occasional touches like the "hospital procession of negro cupids, several headless and all cripples," which Mr. Lorry notices framing the mirror in his hotel (or the whitewashed cupid "in the coolest linen" on the ceiling of his Paris office, which makes its appearance three hundred pages later). But for the most part one goes to the book for qualities which are easier to praise than to illustrate or examine: a rapid tempo which never lets up from the opening sentence, and a sombre eloquence which saves Carton from mere melodrama, and stamps an episode like the running-down of the child by the Marquis's carriage on one's mind with a primitive intensity rarely found after Dickens's early novels, like an outrage committed in a fairy-tale.

But it must be admitted that the *Tale* is in many ways a thin and uncharacteristic work, bringing the mounting despair of the eighteen-fifties to a dead end rather than ushering in the triumphs of the 'sixties. In no other novel, not even *Hard Times,* has Dickens's natural profusion been so drastically pruned. Above all, the book is notoriously deficient in humour. One falls—or flops—back hopefully on the Crunchers, but to small avail. True, the comic element parodies the serious action: Jerry, like his master, is a "Resurrection-Man," but on the only occasion that we see him rifling a grave it turns out to be empty, while his son's panic-stricken flight with an imaginary coffin in full pursuit is nightmarish rather than funny. As comic characters the Crunchers are forced and mechanical; such true humour as there is in the book is rather to be found in scattered observations, but settings and characters are colourful rather than grotesque. Obviously Dickens's humour is many things, but it is usually bound up with a sense of almost magical power over nature: to distort, exaggerate, yoke together or dissolve is to manipulate and control external reality. In Dickens people are always taking on the qualities of objects with which they come into contact, and *vice versa:* a basic Dickensian trick of style, which makes its appearance as early as the opening pages of *Sketches by Boz,* where there is a fine passage ("Our Parish," Chapter VII) on the "resemblance and sympathy" between a man's face and the knocker on his front door. Such transformations are not unknown in *A Tale of Two Cities*—there is the obstinate door at Tellson's with the weak rattle in its throat, for example—but they occur less frequently than in any other Dickens novel, and there is a corresponding lack of power for which a neatly constructed plot is small compensation.

Contrary to what might be expected, this absence of burlesque is accompanied by a failure to present society in any depth. *A Tale of Two Cities* may deal with great political events, but nowhere else in the later work of Dickens is there less sense of society as a living organism. Evrémondes and Defarges alike seem animated by sheer hatred; we hear very little of the stock social themes, money, hypocrisy, and snobbery. Tellson's, musty and cramped and antiquated, makes an excellent Dickensian set-piece, but it is scarcely followed up. Jarvis Lorry, too, is a sympathetic version of the fairy-godfather, a saddened Cheeryble who repines at spending his days "turning a vast pecuniary mangle," but this side of his character is only lightly sketched in. He may glance through the iron bars of his office-window "as if they were ruled for figures too, and everything under the clouds were a sum," but he is more important as a protective, reassuring figure: in times of revolution Tellson's mustiness becomes a positive virtue.

The lack of social density shows up Dickens's melodrama to disadvantage. This is partly a question of length, since in a short novel everything has to be worked in as best it can: Barsad will inevitably turn out to be Miss Pross's long-lost brother, Defarge has to double as Doctor Manette's old servant, and so forth. But there is a deeper reason for feeling more dissatisfaction with the artificial plot here than one does with equally far-fetched situations elsewhere in Dickens. Where society is felt as an all-enveloping force, Dickens is able to turn the melodramatic conventions which he inherited to good use; however preposterous the individual coincidences, they serve an important symbolic function. The world is more of a piece than we suppose, Dickens is saying, and our fates are bound up, however cut off from one another we may appear: the pestilence from Tom-all-Alone's really will spread to the Dedlock mansion, and sooner or later the river in which Gaffer Hexam fishes for corpses will flow through the Veneering drawing-room. In a word, we can't have Miss Havisham without Magwitch. But without a thick social atmosphere swirling round them, the characters of *A Tale of Two Cities* stand out in stark melodramatic isolation; the spotlight is trained too sharply on the implausibilities of the plot, and the stage is set for Sir John Martin-Harvey and *The Only Way*. So, too, the relentless workings of destiny are stressed rather clumsily by such a bare presentation; Madame Defarge points the finger of fate a little too vigorously, and there is a tendency towards heavy repetitions and parallelisms, brought out by the chapter-headings, "A Hand at Cards" and "The Game Made," "Dusk" and "Darkness," and so forth.

Yet despite the dark mood in which it was conceived, the *Tale* isn't a wholly gloomy work; nor is the final impression which it leaves with us one of a wallow of self-pity on the scaffold. We are told of Darnay in the condemned cell (or is it Carton?) that

> his hold on life was strong, and it was very, very hard to loosen; by gradual efforts and degrees unclosed a little here, it clenched the tighter there; and when he brought his strength to bear on that hand and it yielded, this was closed again. There was a hurry, too, in all his thoughts, a turbulent and heated working of his heart, that contended against resignation. (Bk. III, Ch. 13.)

And near the end, as Miss Pross grapples with Madame Defarge, Dickens speaks of "the vigorous tenacity of love, always so much stronger than hate." The gruesome events of the book scarcely bear out such a judgment, yet as an article of faith, if not as a statement of the literal truth, it is curiously impressive. For all the sense of horror which he must have felt stirring within him when he wrote *A Tale of Two Cities,* Dickens remained a moralist and a preacher, and it was his saving strength. But if the author doesn't succumb with Carton, neither does he escape with Darnay. At the end of the book "we" gallop away not to safety and Lucie, but to the false hopes of Pip, the thwarted passion of Bradley Headstone, the divided life of John Jasper. Nothing is concluded, and by turning his malaise into a work of art Dickens obtains parole, not release: the prison will soon be summoning him once more.

From *The Flint and the Flame*

by Earle Davis

Between the writing of *Little Dorrit* and of *A Tale of Two Cities* several important personal experiences affected Dickens' creative attitude. *A Tale of Two Cities* is a completely different kind of novel from any he had previously attempted, to a certain extent unlike his usual composition. It is odd that because this is the Dickens work that has been generally assigned for reading, generations of high school students have known Dickens mainly through this untypical novel. *Great Expectations* is also representative of experimental narrative technique, somewhat unlike his previous custom. One must look to Dickens' life for some light on this shift from the complex, interlocking-plot method and the careful dependence on symbolic reference he had developed in the great novels of his dark period.

When he broke with his wife and got involved in disagreement with the backers of *Household Words*, he decided to start a new magazine. *All the Year Round* needed to establish itself in the public eye, and it had to attract subscribers. It was natural for him to feel commercial pressure and to desire to re-establish his reputation with the reading public. He decided to write a novel for the new magazine which would "sell," and he wanted a subject which would attract attention. He would have to write it in weekly installments, and he recalled how much trouble he had experienced with his panoramic plan in *Hard Times*. Therefore he abandoned the multiple-plot technique and chose a subject completely different from his usual concerns. Accordingly, he did not aim at anything like the breadthwise cutting attempted by Tolstoi in *War and Peace* or by Thomas Hardy in *The Dynasts,* as one might have expected from the example of *Bleak House* and *Little Dorrit.*

From The Flint and the Flame: The Artistry of Charles Dickens, *by Earle Davis (Columbia: University of Missouri Press, 1963), Chapter XII, "Recalled to Life" pp. 238–54. Copyright © 1963 by The Curators of the University of Missouri. Reprinted by permission of The University of Missouri Press. [This is the excerpted central section of the chapter, with some introductory and transitional remarks omitted.]*

His usual rule for aiming at commercial success in fiction was to emphasize excitement, sentiment, and humor. Yet nothing was certain, and you could not foretell success or failure. He had reached sudden fame with *Pickwick,* had sold in the neighborhood of 100,000 copies for each issue of *The Old Curiosity Shop,* had dropped down to 20,000 for *Martin Chuzzlewit,* had gone back up with *Dombey and Son,* had fallen with *David Copperfield,* and had reached about 35,000 for *Bleak House* and *Little Dorrit.* Several conclusions derive from these figures. One of them is that his public did not comprehend the theses of his novels; his violent attacks on Victorian society did not materially affect his popularity and the money he received. A second conclusion is that his mature artistry was not generally understood or appreciated, since his most popular books sold best for reasons which were ephemeral or illogical. *Martin Chuzzlewit* and *David Copperfield* made him the least money of all his novels in monthly part form. From a commercial standpoint it is easy to see that Dickens might have been puzzled about his relationship to his audience. It is certain that his language, his tone, and his choice of material were influenced many times by his efforts to adjust his fiction to his readers, not only from a financial but from an artistic standpoint. Therefore he wrote *A Tale of Two Cities,* his latest attempt to compose a "popular" novel.

The new book was to be "historical." His only previous experimentation with history had been in *Barnaby Rudge.* But this time he was vitally interested in the history and convinced of its importance in relation to his own times. A number of sources supplied the inspiration for his story of the French Revolution. In the background for these influences was Carlyle's *French Revolution,* which Dickens claimed to have read over and over. In this book he felt he had a perfect source book for the primary historical scenes and events he would need.

His basic plot idea derived from the play written by Wilkie Collins, *The Frozen Deep.* The action of this play centers upon rivalry in love, one man at the last sacrificing himself to save the life of the other, who has won the girl. The main characters are Richard Wardour, Frank Aldersley, and Lucy Crayford. When Lucy decides to marry Frank, Richard volunteers for a dangerous sea voyage to the frozen North, and later Frank is assigned to the same expedition. When the exploring party is shipwrecked and marooned, two of the survivors are chosen by lot to attempt to get back to civilization and bring aid. Richard and Frank are—naturally—the two chosen. Frank becomes exhausted, and it appears that Richard may leave him to die. The final scene, however, shows Richard carrying his rival to safety, after which Richard collapses and dies. Dickens acted the role of Richard, and

Collins was Frank in the performance which brought Ellen Ternan eventually into Dickens' life.

The idea of one man sacrificing himself for another who had won the girl beloved of both also implied that the better man deserved the girl. Dickens had often studied the character who did not make the most of his capacities: Martin Chuzzlewit, Steerforth, Richard Carstone, and Henry Gowan show weakness in overcoming their environmental obstacles. Out of this type evolved Sidney Carton, man of great ability and charm, drifting with the tide, but atoning for his weaknesses by a grand gesture at the last—sacrificing himself that the girl he loves might be happy with the man she marries, the man whose life he saves at the cost of his own. Dickens was correct; this kind of story would sell.

The Frozen Deep does not resemble *A Tale of Two Cities* except for the central triangle-sacrifice theme. Dickens took this idea and set it in the time and events of the French Revolution. His main inspiration for the transposition was a novel by Bulwer-Lytton called *Zanoni,* which had been published in 1845. *Zanoni* is full of Rosicrucian dogma and concerns the initiate who has achieved earthly immortality; he lives for centuries. One of the requirements for reaching this magical state is the renunciation of all earthly passions, including love. Zanoni falls in love with a beautiful singer, Viola, and is faced with the choice between temporary happiness and earthly immortality. The theme of the novel is Zanoni's passion; he eventually sacrifices his own life to save Viola's, although she dies too and makes his attempt unavailing.

The early events of *Zanoni* take place in Italy, but the action moves to Paris and the Revolution for its climax. Here Viola is sentenced to the guillotine, and all efforts to help her prove abortive. Suspense rises as Zanoni realizes that the only way to save her is to die for her. Since he is theoretically able to live forever if he will abandon her, he has to make the supreme gesture to prove his love. His substitution for her in the condemned group is relatively simple. The number to die is eighty. Zanoni takes Viola's place and attempts to arrange the disguise and forged passports for her escape with Glyndon, a young man who also loves her. Zanoni then goes to his death by guillotine:

On to the Barrière du Trone. It frowns dark in the air,—the giant instrument of murder! One after one to the glaive,—another and another and another! Mercy! Oh, mercy! is the bridge between the sun and the shade so brief,—brief as a sigh? There, there! *His* turn has come. "Die not yet; leave me not behind. Hear me, hear me!" shrieked the inspired sleeper. "What! and thou smilest still!" They smiled—those pale lips— and *with* the smile, the place of doom, the headsman, the horror vanished! With that smile, all space seemed suffused in eternal sunshine. Up from the earth he rose; he hovered over her,—a thing not of matter, —an IDEA of joy and light! Behind, Heaven opened, deep after deep; and the Hosts of Beauty were seen, rank upon rank, afar; and "Welcome," in a myriad melodies broke from your choral multitude, ye People of the Skies,—"Welcome, O purified by sacrifice, and immortal only through the grave,—this it is to die." And radiant amidst the radiant, the IMAGE stretched forth its arms, and murmured to the sleeper, "Companion of Eternity! This it is to die!"

Comparison with Dickens' eventual death scene for Carton is interesting indeed; the younger author must have wanted to surpass this stylistic monstrosity, and he rose to the occasion.

The Frozen Deep and *Zanoni* combined to provide in the creative mind of Dickens the sacrifice of one lover for another, with the French Revolution and the guillotine providing the scene for death. When Dickens began planning the action which would lead up to this climax, he must have felt that a more dramatic means of substituting one lover for the other would have to be worked out. Previous novelists, including Collins, had written stories in which one main character resembled the other, resulting in confusion. Collins had just done this in *Hide and Seek,* and he was to do it in *The Woman in White* soon afterward. So Dickens seized upon the idea of having Darnay and Carton resemble each other.

The fact that Collins had been writing stories about the French Revolution had something to do with turning Dickens to this historical background. Two of these tales, *Gabriel's Marriage* and *Sister Rose,* were printed in *Household Words.* The latter tale introduces characters named Trudaine and Sister Rose who are denounced by Rose's villainous husband because they aided the escape of a victim of the revolutionary party. They are tried, sentenced, and would have gone to their deaths but for the help of a certain Lomaque, a worthless character who atones for his shameless life by saving them. He does it by painting an erasing liquid over their names on the death list, timing this to coincide with the fall of Robespierre, when all prisoners were released. Lomaque is a spy, and like Barsad in *A Tale of Two Cities,* he is in a position to effect a substitution of prisoners before the march to the guillotine. Dickens got Barsad into his novel early, because he knew he would have to supply a convincing way of putting Carton in Darnay's place at the climax. The general nature of this inspiration from Collins is apparent.

With a broad sketch of his proposed novel securely set in his mind, Dickens had a few definite ideas for narration: sacrifice of one lover for another; substitution before the guillotine; the French Revolution as his scene. He needed a reason for his hero's being sentenced to die.

Those who died were generally aristocrats; Darnay becomes an aristocrat, but a good one. He accordingly disagrees with the evil principles of his class, principles which Carlyle had categorically insisted caused the Revolution, and long before the Terror, Darnay emigrates to England. This allowed Dickens to balance the action between the two countries, and his idea for his title followed naturally. Darnay could fall in love in England, win his suit for Lucy against Carton, and later be caught in the Terror's net in Paris, setting up the closing scenes.

At what point his actual reference to Carlyle occurred does not matter for our purposes. Perhaps it was previous to some of the points discussed or coincident with them. Carlyle does not tell lurid stories of the atrocious deeds of the aristocrats in the days before the Revolution. Dickens understood the conclusions of Carlyle very well. Lack of concern, pity, brains, understanding, and leadership among the aristocrats had driven the downtrodden lower classes to rise in desperation. Any ruling class needed to pay more than it was *forced* to pay in wages or living conditions for its underlings, or it courted revolt. This point had been the essence of Carlyle's warnings in *Chartism* and *Past and Present*. But for his story Dickens needed a striking example of the criminal incapacity and intolerance of the ruling classes.

When he asked for help in discussing his proposed tale with Carlyle, the latter confused his own scholarly practice with Dickens' simple needs and sent down a cartload of books which he had used in preparing *The French Revolution*. These books must have looked very imposing and uninviting to the novelist, but he selected from them the ones he thought would do him the most good. Forster says that Dickens found Mercier's *Tableau de Paris* a useful source for many incidents and ideas incorporated in the novel. Actually, all Dickens got from it was an atrocity or two.

Mercier provided a meticulous rendition of the years which preceded the Revolution. His several-volume history covered the entire story and gave Carlyle important parts of his data. Among Mercier's facts and rumors of fact were instances of the feudal privileges once held by the lord over his serfs. These included the notorious custom which permitted the lord to take temporarily any woman in his domain from her family or husband, the so-called *droit du seigneur*. Many tales have been founded on this custom, particularly when some rebellion occurred against it. The man who refused to give up his newly wed wife was often roughly treated, sometimes tortured or killed when he resisted or attempted vengeance. Dickens decided to use this spectacular example of evil aristocratic privilege in his novel.

Forster pointed out later, when Dickens had supplied it as the reason for Dr. Manette's confinement in the Bastille, that such feudal customs had disappeared long years before the time Dickens covered in *A Tale of Two Cities*. The author seems somewhat nettled in his reply:

> I had of course full knowledge of the formal surrender of the feudal privileges, but these had been bitterly felt quite as near to the time of the Revolution as the Doctor's narrative, which you will remember dates long before the Terror. With the slang of the new philosophy on the one side, it was not unreasonable or unallowable on the other, to suppose a nobleman wedded to the old cruel ideas, and representing the time going out as his nephew represents the time coming in. If there be anything certain on earth, I take it that the condition of the French peasant generally at that day was intolerable. No later inquiries or provings by figures will hold water against the tremendous tesimony of men living at that time. There is a curious book printed at Amsterdam, written to make out no case whatever, and tiresome enough in its literal dictionary-like minuteness; scattered up and down the pages of which is full authority for my marquis. This is Mercier's *Tableau de Paris*.

In Carlyle's history, as part of his description of the fall of the Bastille, there is reprinted a letter found in the paper archives of the old prison. Dated October 7, 1752, it reads:

> If for my consolation Monseigneur would grant me, for the sake of God and the Most Blessed Trinity, that I could have news of my dear wife; were it only her name on a card, to show she is alive! It were the greatest consolation I could receive; and I should forever bless the greatness of Monseigneur.

This letter intrigued Dickens. It became his device for revealing the secret of Dr. Manette's imprisonment, elaborated into an account of the whole story of the woman appropriated by Monseigneur, brought to death along with her protesting brother. Dr. Manette, called in a medical capacity to attend the dying woman and her brother, later writes a letter to the King about what he had seen, and is therefore put in the Bastille by Monseigneur through a *lettre de cachet*. The letter quoted by Carlyle furnishes the ending of Dr. Manette's document, found by Defarge in Manette's empty cell in the Bastille when it is stormed:

> If it had pleased God to put it in the hard heart of either of the brothers, in all these frightful years, to grant me any tidings of my dearest wife—so much as to let me know by a word whether alive or dead—I might have thought that He had not quite abandoned them.

Mention of the prisoner's wife suggests the existence of a child. Dickens needed the girl for whom Carton would die. What better idea than that she should be Dr. Manette's child, sent to England after her mother's death and her father's imprisonment, ignorant of his fate?

That Darnay, nephew of Monseigneur and son of the brother who was involved in the affair which led to Dr. Manette's imprisonment, should also go to England, love and marry Lucy Manette, appealed to Dickens as another dramatic source of emotion. This circumstance would set the stage for Manette's Parisian and revolutionary friends to take revenge on all the descendants of Monseigneur for his past evil deeds, and it would provide the excuse for Darnay's death sentence.

In planning his novel, Dickens also took account of the difficulties he had previously encountered in the shorter installments. His solution was a simple one, but he had never tried it before: long novel—complex plots; short novel—one plot. All he really needed was the Darnay-Manette-Carton intrigue, with a dependent subplot to provide for the detail of exchanging his principals in prison before the guillotine. This is where Barsad came in, the spy whose scheme to fake the death of his fellow spy, Roger Cly, would be discovered by Jerry Cruncher, the body snatcher. Later in Paris this information is used by Carton to put pressure on Barsad and force his help in replacing Darnay with Carton on the guillotine list. A further narrative device occurred to Dickens in adapting his tale to shorter installments. This idea was to eliminate excessive dialogue, change his practice of developing his story by conversation, and describe more of the action. Forster did not like this idea at all. He says:

> To rely less upon character than upon incident, and to resolve that his actors should be expressed by the story more than they should express themselves by dialogue, was for him a hazardous, and can hardly be called an entirely successful, experiment.

The result, however hazardous it seemed to Forster, did contribute one thing to the final effect: It automatically eliminated many opportunities for melodramatic excesses, and by substituting description Dickens produced a tighter, faster-moving story than usual. What he lost was characteristic humor and entertaining speech. He had difficulty in selecting the scenes he wished to use from the many which occurred to him. He did not like restraint. He complains in his letters, "the small portions drive me frantic," but he was interested in the story and in the possibilities of his tragic action: "Nothing but the interest of the subject, and the pleasure of striving with the difficulty of the form of treatment . . . could else repay the time and trouble of the incessant condensation."

To the modern reader Dickens' way of developing all his novels is dramatic, since he normally uses dialogue more than any other device and designs his scenes as if for the stage. For *A Tale of Two Cities* he planned the course of action in direct imitation of the way it would be done for the theater, even though he had resolved to limit his dialogue.

He says: "How as to a story in two periods—with a lapse of time between, like a French Drama?" The reference to French drama is significant. He was thinking of the type of French tragedy which started
its action with a prologue before the main acts, the conflict of motives
being seized at some interesting point, back action thereby revealed,
and the stage prepared for the main intrigue. The action which followed was usually in two acts which were carefully balanced in effect.
Dickens decided to use as a kind of prologue the journey of Mr. Lorry
to France to bring to England the recently released prisoner, Dr.
Manette, to restore him to his daughter who had grown up in safety
in England while he was confined in the Bastille. This opening scene
introduced the mystery of what the doctor had done to cause his confinement. Then Dickens was ready to leap into his main story. *A Tale
of Two Cities* is divided into three books as it is printed, but the first
is really the prologue, shorter than the other two, which are balanced
in length and action.

The practice of the historical novelist requires some specific knowl-
edge of the history involved. Carlyle is Dickens' authority for the
scenes in Paris before and during the Terror. There are three kinds of
inspiration in the references Dickens makes to Carlyle. These are
direct borrowings of description and scene, indirect use of characters
and events, and suggestions which Dickens transfers to different characters or combines into new forms for fictional purposes.

For example, in the section in which the Bastille is stormed Dickens
transposes many of Carlyle's own words:

> . . . the living sea rose, wave on wave, depth on depth, and overflowed
> the city to that point. Alarm-bells ringing, drums beating, the sea
> raging and thundering on its new beach, the attack begun . . .

> . . . behold, . . . how the multitude flows on, welling through every
> street; tocsin furiously pealing, all drums beating the *générale:* the
> Suburb Saint-Antoine rolling hitherward wholly, as one man! . . .

The second example is Carlyle's. The historical source gives many
details which Dickens omits or concentrates, but the entire description
is quite similar up to Defarge's journey to Dr. Manette's old cell to
hunt for the document hidden there—the document which will later
doom Darnay at the time of his trial.

Further direct borrowings are evident in the following chapter,
which tells of continued killings and hangings to the *lanternes.* The
murder of old Foullon who had once been injudicious enough to say
of the third estate, "Let them eat grass!" is similar in both books.
Smaller resemblances are numerous. Carlyle always talks of the suburb
of Saint-Antoine as a sort of symbol of the third estate. It is here that
the worst rioters, known as Brigands, operate. Dickens naturally puts

the Defarges and their wine shop in this section. The conduct of the trials, prison procedures, the tumbrils, and the guillotine come from Carlyle. The dancing of the Carmagnole finds its place in the novel as Lucy watches the prison where her husband lies. When Darnay is temporarily released he puts his name over the door of his residence in accord with the custom noted by Carlyle. The third volume of *The French Revolution* was an extremely convenient source book for all the details Dickens needed, and the novel gives the effect of authenticity for this reason.

Defarge and his wife come indirectly from Carlyle. The history presents Santerre, a brewer, living in Saint-Antoine, who became a leader of the revolt, and Carlyle makes casual mention of the president of the Jacobin Society, whose name was Lafarge. A certain Usher Maillard was active in the storming of the Bastille, doing most of what Defarge did in Dickens' narrative. "Defarge" combines from these originals whatever the novelist needed for his action. Carlyle also devoted eleven chapters in his history of the early rioting to "The Insurrection of the Women." One of his female leaders, a black Joan of Arc, was Demoiselle Théroigne, a striking and spectacular mob captain. In the fight at the Tuileries, Carlyle describes her as *Sibyl* Théroigne: "Vengeance, *Victoire ou la mort!*" Mme. Defarge is not "small-waisted," but she performs as mob leader, being much more ruthless than her husband. Dickens also invents a character, a companion of Mme. Defarge, whom he designates only as The Vengeance. He took what he wanted from Carlyle, changed and concentrated, it, and dressed up the details of his story from the historical record.

Carlyle attributes the worst excesses of the mob to the Jacobins, or the *Jacquerie*. Dickens creates types of revolt leaders from the lowest classes, giving them the names of Jacques One, Jacques Two, Jacques Three. The insignia of the French Revolution was patterned in threes —witness the tricolor and the slogan, "Liberty, Fraternity, and Equality." The Jacobin women were especially prominent at the guillotine, too, and the stories of their knitting while watching the executions were famous. Carlyle describes them at the executions, and Dickens applies this graphic bit of data to Mme. Defarge's knitted record of victims, handwork in which the names of the doomed were entwined with vengeance in her own variety of shorthand. The women are there knitting when Carton dies.

Names occasionally wander from one book to the other, perhaps in some entirely different connection from the original, showing merely that the name remained in Dickens' mind and was appropriated because the novelist needed some kind of cognomen. The hated *gabelle*, France's salt tax, turns up as the name of Darnay's agent on Monseigneur's estate, the man whose letter to Darnay begging his assistance in his trial is the excuse for tempting Darnay back to France and his capture. Carlyle casually mentions Thelusson's Bank, where the great Necker was once a clerk. Dickens, needing a name for the agency which served to bring Lucy Manette and later her father from France to England, shifted the establishment to Tellson's Bank, with branches in Paris as well as London.

Carlyle's description of the butchery which went on outside La Force Prison in the September Massacres of 1792 is about as horrible as anything in his chamber of hyperbolic horrors. Wanton and brutal slaying in the streets with axe and sword is much more forthright than death under the guillotine. Dickens describes the great grindstone in the yard outside the quarters of Tellson's Bank in Paris where the mob, shirts and clothing dripping with the blood of their victims, comes to sharpen weapons blunted in the awful slaughter.

Much of this transposition is the routine custom of the historical novelist, taking his details from a reputable source and supplying his facts where they are needed in his story. Of more interest to the critic of narrative technique are the instances in which only a suggestion is in the source, Dickens' expansion adding to the picture or the characterization which becomes an important part of his story. Dr. Manette, for example, lost his mind in the long years of confinement. He learned the shoemaker's trade in prison, and although nursed back to health and sanity upon coming to England, he suffers lapses of memory and reverts to his prison occupation whenever he is seriously troubled. This regression happens when Lucy marries Darnay and again when all seems lost and Darnay is sentenced to die.

Louis XVI was the king who mismanaged the governmental treatment of all parties in the days before the Terror. Without ability at the proper moment, he was often a pitiable figure as he became more and more enmeshed in problems beyond his scope. Occasionally he escaped from the world of his troubles with the tools of a smith, finding perfect release and forgetfulness while fashioning something purely mechanical. The leap from this account in Carlyle to Dickens' brilliant use of the shoemaker's tools by Dr. Manette shows his genius in action; it is the trait which makes Dr. Manette the unforgettable person he is.

The whole picture of Carton's death is traceable to bits of inspiration from Carlyle. Maton de la Varenne tells of his own narrow escape from death when the haphazard trials were at their height. His terror and the wild events during the time he spent in prison are recounted in a pamphlet called "Ma Résurrection." Dickens seized upon the idea of the resurrection as a symbol for Carton's death and intensified it in other parts of the story. The connection with Christ's death and the doctrine of the atonement was an easy transference. Dickens prepares for his use of the resurrection theme by having Carton remember, on the night before Darnay is sentenced, how he had followed his father to the grave, and the preacher had read: "I am the resurrection and the life."

Mme. Roland, a brave and noble lady, was another individual sentenced to die. Carlyle tells her story:

> And now, short preparation soon done, she too shall go her last road. There went with her a certain Lamarche, "Director of Assignat-printing"; whose dejection she endeavoured to cheer. Arrived at the foot of the scaffold, she asked for pen and paper, "to write the strange thoughts that were rising in her"; a remarkable request; which was refused. Looking at the Statue of Liberty which stands there, she says bitterly: "O Liberty, what things are done in thy name!" For Lamarche's sake, she will die first; show him how easy it is to die: "Contrary to the order," said Samson.—"Pshaw, you cannot refuse the last request of a Lady"; and Samson yielded.

That Dickens referred to this passage is clear from his epilogue, where he records what Sidney Carton might have been thinking had he been able to do what Mme. Roland wanted to do. Says Dickens:

> One of the most remarkable sufferers by the same axe—a woman—had asked at the foot of the same scaffold, not long before, to be allowed to write down the thoughts that were inspiring her. If he had given utterance to his, and they were prophetic, they would have been these: . . .

The thoughts follow, ending with the lines:

> "It is a far, far better thing that I do, than I have ever done; it is a far, far better rest that I go to than I have ever known."

Mme. Roland's friend Lamarche had been timid about dying. The inspired idea of giving Carton the little seamstress to comfort—a completely new character in the story—follows from this hint. There is one other influence. It comes from the account in Carlyle of the manner in which Elizabeth, sister of Louis, and the "once timorous" Marchioness de Crussol went to the scaffold. They embraced before they walked up the steps to the guillotine. And so the little seamstress waits her turn, and as she goes to her death, "she kisses his lips, he kisses hers."

A Tale of Two Cities is the one book of Dickens in which the student can see his artistry in some detail, since the sources can be compared more accurately and completely than usual. His practice of noting and transforming anything he could use shows also to advantage. His climactic chapter depicting the death of Carton is his best experiment with sensation, and it reaches tragic intensity. The curtains of trite melodrama have fallen away; dissection of his narrative devices shows how far he had come from the pure sentimentalism of Little Nell's death.

The novel, excellent as it is in certain respects, presents a number of problems. It is different from Dickens' usual narrative style, and this difference does not utilize every resource which we are accustomed to associate with his artistry. Farce and caricature are either absent or underplayed. The only effective farce character is Jerry Cruncher, the body snatcher who robs graves and objects to his wife's praying while he is at work. Mr. Lorry is described in the old manner of caricature, Mr. Stryver is a stupid ass, and Miss Pross as Lucy's maid has some eccentric moments. No remarkable speech mannerisms are given to any of the characters, unless Jerry may be considered to have one. In a sense Dr. Manette's "far away" voice is such a device, and it is appropriate to his long confinement in the Bastille. The development of action by dialogue is not completely replaced by description, for there are a few rare moments when Dickens reverts to his old habits. Examples are the scenes in which Jerry talks to his wife, or Carton almost proposes to Lucy.

The development of the plot is generally expert. In Book Two Dickens alternates action between England and France, managing to balance the events which introduce the Defarges and the scene in which Monseigneur is assassinated after he has run over a child, with the story of Lucy and Dr. Manette in London, building up to Lucy's marriage with Darnay. Dickens also carefully contrasts the two trials for Darnay's life, the first showing him acquitted on the false charge of spying brought by Barsad and Cly. Carton saves him by calling attention to the remarkable resemblance they have for each other, and thus confuses the witness and the jury. The second trial, in Book Three, gives Carton another opportunity for saving Darnay, but only after sentence is passed.

The weaknesses of the novel derive partially from Dickens' need to have something exciting happen in each installment. It is a shock to read the Bastille chapter and find the authentic surging action come to its crest when Defarge goes to Dr. Manette's cell. It is almost as if, for the purposes of the plot, the whole taking of the Bastille is important only because a fatal private document is hidden there. This is a question of emphasis, yet the novel is the tale of Carton, Darnay, and Lucy, not of the larger implications of the Revolution itself. In his dark novels Dickens had used his plots to illuminate the largest issues he could imagine. In this book he does not try to make the story of the Manettes symbolize the deepest meanings of French history.

Wilkie Collins was not quite satisfied with the way in which Dickens handled his plot. In addition to suggesting that the story of Dr. Manette might be revealed early, he apparently felt that the device of the document which leads to the conviction of Darnay was weak or unlikely. Perhaps the doctor might have been able to write such a detailed and lengthy account of his wrongs and secrete it in his cell; it is improbable that the entire record would be read in the trial at this date in Paris. Dickens certainly imitated the practice of French drama in his alternating trial sequence, in which the hero's concerns prosper at first, then are suddenly reversed. Stage and motion-picture versions of the double trial usually combine events of the two days and speed up the action. In this and in several other moments which develop Dickens' intrigue there is the suggestion of overelaborate complication.

A few sequences have little motivation. Why does Carton go to Paris? Darnay goes to help Gabelle escape a death sentence, although what happens to Gabelle is lost in Darnay's own difficulties. Carton supposedly goes because Lucy is in trouble. Of course, Darnay spends a long time in prison before his trial, Dickens rapidly passing over months in his narrative. Carton could hardly know when he leaves London that he will be called upon to sacrifice his life for Darnay. In this kind of novel, such coincidence is generally accepted by the average reader, but it must be taken into account by the particular and critical ones.

The substitution of Carton for Darnay calls for more manipulation. Dickens' readers would hardly retain respect for Darnay if he easily permitted Carton to die for him; therefore he must be tricked into escaping. Dickens solved this problem by having Darnay drugged with some form of anesthetic so that he will be far from Paris before he wakens to learn what has happened. The exact nature of the anesthetic remains doubtful, since such drugs were not in general use at the time. Dickens reached into the misty realm of alchemy to find the mysterious potion which could secure the necessary effect. This point is easily accepted by the modern reader because he is used to the general properties of anesthesia and knows about Mickey Finns from modern detective novels.

The symbolism used by Dickens in this novel is of a different order from the fog of *Bleak House* and the prison atmosphere of *Little Dorrit*. It centers about the "recalled to life" hint in Carlyle and extends itself to the general implication of resurrection. Dr. Manette's release is a form of resurrection, and "Recalled to Life" is the password of the Prologue or Book One. Jerry Cruncher introduces a grotesque variation of this theme when he steals bodies to sell to medical students. Carton's death is a form of spiritual resurrection at the same time that

Darnay's release is to life from the sentence of death. Carton also carries some sense of atonement into his sacrifice, and the symbol works its way into the great climax.

This climax is prepared for and built up in a more concise fashion than in any other novel. The last three chapters are chronologically adjusted for this effect. In Chapter XIII Carton substitutes himself for Darnay, and the drugged man is hurried from the city by Mr. Lorry, Lucy, and Dr. Manette. Enough is told to assure the reader that they escape, and then they are lost to the narrative. Chapter XIV recounts the death of Mme. Defarge at the hands of Miss Pross, then goes on to show that she and Jerry Cruncher escape too. In Chapter XV Carton goes to the guillotine, and that is the end. In other novels Dickens had sometimes added chapters and incidents to take care of the future of almost every character in the story. In *A Tale of Two Cities* Carton dies, and the story is finished except for his imaginary thoughts at the scaffold.

The thesis of the novel is: *Revolution can happen in England too!* The aristocrats in France were stupid and hardhearted; they were responsible for spurring the people to revolt; England's ruling classes were also being stupid and hardhearted. Dickens joins with Carlyle in showing the reasons for what had happened in France, although he does not try to bring in a panoramic view of historical characters like Mirabeau, Lafayette, Robespierre, or Napoleon. Nor is there any attempt to do what Tolstoi might have attempted: show the struggles of the government for money in time of depression, the difficulties of parliament, the pathetic story of Marie Antoinette, the philosophical thinking behind the movement. Dickens centered on saying of the French Revolution just what he had said concerning the economic crises which were happening in England. In the first part of his novel he sympathizes with the downtrodden people; but at the last these people are the villains. Extreme injustice leads to violence; see what happened in the days of the Terror. If British employers insist upon the selfish laissez-faire doctrine, workers will eventually rise to protect themselves. A catastrophe like the French Revolution could easily happen elsewhere.

The implied comparison is not quite valid. Modern research shows that the French Revolution was a much more complex affair than Carlyle and Dickens judged. But the effect of Dickens' novel is intentionally limited in scope. The book is not *War and Peace*. His tale remains the account of one small group of characters who suffered in the course of the cataclysm which surged about them and went on to historical, political, and economic developments completely beyond the purposes of the tale. On a small and relatively selective scale within the limits defined it is a dynamic historical novel, even though it does not call upon all the technical resources at Dickens' command. He sacrificed solidity for the spectacular, the large scene for the single vivid flash, but he got it.

The Method of *A Tale of Two Cities*

by William H. Marshall

"Knitted, in her own stitches, and her own symbols, it will always be as plain to her as the sun." So Ernest Defarge describes the meaning which his wife imposes upon her art. We are tempted at first to regard the words as a description of Dickens's method in *A Tale of Two Cities,* but in the novel the result is far more subtle than a private allegory. It is commonplace to recognize the popularity of this work, the difference between it and other Dickens novels, and the successful use of what would usually be hackneyed devices, such as the opening with a lost-and-found scene, with which many novels close, and the closing with a switch of doubles, with which many open. Prolepsis and antithesis are characteristically associated with Dickens's method, but here we have a pattern involving the explicit and obvious use of these for structural purposes and the implicit and indefinite use for symbolic purposes. In the fusion of these we find the method of *A Tale of Two Cities.*

There are many obvious parallelisms in the novel, which because of the restricted number of characters, never become confusing or distracting. The contrast is explicit in the title, as in the opening chapter, "It was the best of times, it was the worst of times" (I, i). Mr. Lorry's journey to Paris and his recall of Dr. Manette to life in the beginning of the story foretell the flight from Paris and the rescue of Charles Darnay toward the end. Darnay's one trial in London foreshadows the two in Paris. The First Book ends with Dr. Manette's release from prison and the Second with Darnay's beginning the journey that will lead him to prison. The differences are as obvious as the similarities in a comparison between Mr. Lorry's professional activities and Jerry Cruncher's other trade. Manette and Darnay, both Frenchmen, the principal persons "Recalled to life," present a kind of

"*The Method of* A Tale of Two Cities," *by William H. Marshall. From* The Dickensian, *LVII, part 3, no. 335 (September, 1961), 183–89. Copyright © 1961 by* The Dickensian. *Reprinted by permission of* The Dickensian. [*This article appears in modified form as a part of Chapter VII of the author's book,* The World of the Victorian Novel *(South Brunswick and New York: A. S. Barnes and Co., Inc.; London: Thomas Yoseloff, Ltd., 1967).*]

opposition which becomes comprehensible only as the story unfolds; and Lorry and Carton, the recallers to life, represent mutually exclusive areas in the British character. Dr. Manette and Sydney Carton are both concerned with fusing the split personality. And always there is present the comparison between the mob of London and the mob of Paris and, derivatively, between the few and the many.

These more easily recognized parallelisms are usually structural, that is, they are concerned with the action of the work and in themselves may frequently be meaningless. It is, however, those parallelisms which are part of the descriptions, the themes, and the moods of *A Tale of Two Cities,* those which are implicit in the work as an artistic creation, frequently possessing limited structural value, which give the work the basis of its appeal and its power. They are essential to the full meaning of the novel, but because of their nature and function—they constitute a complex of symbolism rather than sheer allegory—the full meaning is indefinite, elusive, and uncertain.

To pursue this line of criticism with regard to *A Tale of Two Cities* may be to suggest to many readers that Dickens is here more profound or complex—more "metaphysical" or "poetic"—in his meaning than they have been accustomed to admit. This is certainly not my intention, but it is apparent that many readers have sacrificed the image of Dickens as a thinking being and a conscious artist to the insistence on his commonplace practicality. They have confused the quality of the point of view, obvious and somewhat simple, which Dickens establishes for his readers, with the craft that he employs, subtle and at times complex, to develop such a point of view. Regarded objectively, *David Copperfield* may be taken to have a meaning, that simple goodness and intelligence ultimately bring happiness; or *A Tale of Two Cities* may convey the proposition that love conquers hate. Both are simple meanings, but their nature does not require that the method of projecting them, of constructing the novels through which they are presented, need also be simple. Reduced to a statement, the objective meaning of *A la Recherche du Temps perdu* or *Portrait of the Artist as a Young Man* may be quite simple, but few, if any, would suggest that the method of Proust or of Joyce is simple. The comment of Professors Wellek and Warren on the results of analysis of philosophic content is as applicable to novels as to poetry: "we frequently discover mere commonplaces concerning man's mortality or the uncertainty of fate."

Such is the case of *A Tale of Two Cities.* The phrase "Recalled to Life," the title of the First Book, reveals at once that the novel is about the relation between life and death, that it embodies the rebirth theme. The developing situation involves the desire of a people for political and social regeneration, and the principal characters in the novel dramatize the means by which love alone can bring about rebirth. Dr. Manette is the first "recalled to life." Then Charles Darnay is once "recalled" from death under English Law and twice under French Terror. Throughout the novel the meaning of the phrase is implicit in incidents. Miss Pross discovers her brother alive, and even Madame Defarge is "recalled" in that she reveals herself as the one surviving member of the peasant family injured by the brothers Evrémonde. At all times life and death are juxtaposed to give the structure and meaning of the novel. Related to this juxtaposition is the antithesis between the worlds of reality and of dream—in the chapter "Echoing Footsteps"; in the reference to "the shadows of the actual Bastille thrown upon him [Dr. Manette] by a summer sun, when the substance was three hundred miles away" (II, iv); and in the picture of Darnay, alone in his cell, dreaming that he is home again and yet, when Carton comes to rescue him, incapable of accepting this situation as reality. In terms of the antithesis between reality and dream we grasp the significance of the silent interplay of eyes and hands in the action—the watching and the knitting—of Madame Defarge, for whom reality becomes not the world of flesh which she records in her work, but that record itself. The central dramatic parallelism of the work, the contrast-in-similarity between Charles Darnay and Sydney Carton, fuses the life-death and thence the reality-dream juxtaposition. "Indeed, I begin to think we are not much alike in any particular you and I," Carton remarks to Darnay after the English trial, the outcome of which arose from their apparent similarity (II, iv). Each represents what the other might have been. Carton admits to himself that he dislikes Darnay because "he shows you what you have fallen away from, and what you might have been!" (II, iv). Carton dislikes the image of that with which in life he would but cannot identify himself, that which he can become only in death. The meaning of *A Tale of Two Cities* is concerned with irony, the perceived difference between essence and appearance, in this instance the coming of life from death.

The method of the novel, originating within but transcending the meaning, is the development of the life-death antithesis—with its implication that every object has its shadow and every being its alternate —into a pattern of images, whose value, though frequently structural, is always symbolic; but the significance of the symbol in any given instance is sufficiently inconclusive that the imaginative faculty of the reader, though stimulated to relate this symbol to others in the work, is not inhibited by a fixed allegorical equation. The method of the novel amplifies its meaning: we know that *A Tale of Two Cities* is about rebirth through death, the essential Christian paradox, but we cannot reduce to a simple statement all that it says about this.

The method is most obvious in the opposition between symbols of life and death. These usually take the form of images of food and of destruction. Early in the novel the mill is explicitly the symbol of the system that grinds people unto death rather than of the peaceful production of food; it foretells the appearance of both the grindstone, with which the instruments of slaughter are to be sharpened, and the guillotine itself. And at this same early point we learn that amid hunger, "Nothing was represented in a flourishing condition, save tools and weapons" (I, v). In time, only the conditions of the latter will be "flourishing." But for the moment ferment exists just beneath the surface: "the time was to come, when the gaunt scarecrows of that region should have watched the lamplighter, in their idleness and hunger, so long, as to conceive the idea of improving on his method, and hauling up men by those ropes and pulleys, to flare upon the darkness of their condition" (I, v). In the ceremony of taking chocolate, "the leprosy of unreality disfigured every human creature in attendance upon Monseigneur" (II, vii). The fountain in the country recalls that in the town, and though both would ordinarily be symbols of life, each becomes a scene of death—in the city a child lies under the wheels of the carriage of the Marquis, and much later in the country the body of the murderer of the Marquis remains hanging on the gallows near the fountain. "It is frightful messieurs. How can the women and children draw water! Who can gossip of an evening under that shadow!" remarks the mender of roads to Defarge and the three Jacques. "When I left the village, Monday evening as the sun was going to bed, and looked back from the hill, the shadow struck across the church, across the mill, across the prison—seemed to strike across the earth, messieurs, to where the sky rests upon it!" (II, xv). And in time the shadow becomes reality of course, and the fire that destroys the chateau of the Marquis becomes so intense that "molten lead and iron boiled in the marble basin of the fountain; the water ran dry" (II, xxiii). The massacre "was to set a great mark of blood upon the blessed garnering time of harvest" (III, i). During the second French trial of Darnay, Madame Defarge, looking on the face of the hated one who is to be condemned, is described as "feasting" (III, ix). And the tumbrils, instruments of death, are compared to plows as they cut through the crowds (III, xv). There are other examples, but in all instances the symbols of death seem to triumph over the symbols of life—only to give greater emphasis to the resolution of the work when it comes.

The most significant images of life and death are those of blood, wine, and stone. In the beginning the relation is indicated by the incident of the man writing the word *blood* with wine spilled on the stone before Defarge's shop. "Is there no other place to write such words in?" Defarge asks (I, v). The question is rhetorical, and the answer lies in the remark of one of the three Jacques standing in the wine shop: "It is not often . . . that many of these miserable beasts know the taste of wine, or of anything but black bread and death" (I, v). Wine is traditionally a beneficent symbol, the food for life, as blood is the sustainer of life; but when either is spilled, it becomes a maleficent symbol—of hate, waste, and death—and on this value rests much of the development of the method of the work. The wine mars the stone with what seems to be a death-like permanence, which will not yield to supposedly purifying force of water. Regarding the "terrestrial scheme," Sydney Carton remarks: "As to me, the greatest desire I have, is to forget that I belong to it. It has no good in it for me—except wine like this—nor I for it" (II, iv). His wine, explicitly red wine, recalls that spilled in front of Defarge's shop and foretells the fall of blood, the only means by which Sydney Carton can fulfill his death-wish, but also much more.

The image of stone is potentially the symbol of life, as in the stone used in a mill to grind grain; but through much of the novel stone symbolizes death, at times explicitly so, as in the report of the murder of the Marquis, "that there was one stone face too many, up at the chateau" (II, ix). In the description of the village at night, as the body of the murderer hangs from its scaffold, the life-death symbols as they have appeared to this point are brought together: "Chateau and hut, stone face and dangling figure, the red stain on the stone floor, and the pure water in the village well—thousands of acres of land—a whole province of France—all France itself—lay under the night sky, concentrated into a faint hair-breadth line" (II, xvi). The blood-wine relation is again explicit in the contrast between the security of Lucie's life in England and the threat to her happiness which the mob unconsciously prepares in France: "Now, Heaven defeat the fancy of Lucie Darnay, and keep these feet far out of her life! For, they are headlong, mad, and dangerous; and in the years so long after the breaking of the cask at Defarge's wine-shop door, they are not easily purified when once stained red" (II, xxi). Defarge's shop has become the center for the spilling of blood. The grindstone, anticipated by the mill and foretelling the guillotine in its lifeless substance and deathly function, is a kind of unifying central symbol; as two men turn at it, "some women held wine to their mouths that they might drink; and what with dropping blood, and what with dropping wine, and what with the stream of sparks struck out of the stone, all their wicked atmosphere seemed gore and fire"; in the silence, when the stone was again still, it "stood there in the calm morning air, with a red upon it that the sun had never given and

would never take away" (III, ii). And the blood of the daily group of
her victims is "the day's wine to La Guillotine" (III, xv).

The association of blood and wine is probably archetypal but certainly, within the Christian tradition, orthodox. The Eucharistic suggestions should be quite apparent, despite a possible tendency to
minimize the traditional element in Dickens's own background and
in the culture in which he and his readers lived. But the use of these
images as part of the action would seem to be ironic, for, in immediate
appearances at least, the blood-wine correspondence portends evil—
the stone remains stained. Man's evil, feeding on hatred, would seem
to produce only further evil, and the journey into the shadow of death
would appear to bring no rebirth. But for this thesis of action there is
an antithesis of symbol, first suggested perhaps in the description of
the calm that came to Dr. Manette following the emotional intensity of
his reunion with Lucie—"emblem to humanity, of the rest and silence
into which the storm called Life must hush at last" (I, vi)—and finally
made fully explicit in the presumed thoughts of Sydney Carton in the
moment before death. From the beginning of the work to the conclusion, despite all appearances, the meaning emerges, that ultimately
good and love will destroy evil and hate. To state this as I have done is
to recapitulate the essential teaching of Christian ethics, but it is also
to repeat a cliché: it carries no more emotional force in itself than the
mere assertion that Miss Pross possesses "the vigorous tenacity of love,
always so much stronger than hate" (III, xiv); it is forceful only because it emerges from the story and, more significantly, from the
scheme of images which become the symbols of redemption running
through the novel.

Evil engenders evil; terror creates terror. In Defarge and his wife we
find what has happened to France, what could happen to any nation,
to any man: if we hate, we become what we hate. But eventually
hatred, though intense, is self-destructive, and of this assertion the
image of the rack is an emblem: "the last drop of blood having been
extracted from the flints, and the last screw of the rack having been
turned so often that its purchase crumbled, and it now turned and
turned with nothing to bite" (II, xxiii). Madame Defarge, to be destroyed by her own pistol, so surprises Miss Pross that the English
lady drops the basin in which she has been washing her eyes, and it
"fell to the ground broken, and the water flowed to the feet of
Madame Defarge. By strange stern ways, and through much staining
blood, these feet had come to meet that water" (III, xiv). In the opening lines of the final chapter the narrator remarks, "Crush humanity
out of shape once more, under similar hammers, and it will twist itself
into the same tortured forms." And Carton, about to die, is presumed

to foresee that in years ahead "this place" will be "fair to look upon,
with not a trace of this day's disfigurement" (III, xv).

But before this, as he has resolved upon his plan, Sydney Carton,
the man who would die rather than live but has had the compelling
motivation to do neither, recalls the "solemn words, which had been
read at his father's grave" but now have for him the meaning held
only for the reborn: "I am the resurrection and the life, saith the
Lord: he that believeth in me, though he were dead, yet shall he live:
and whosoever liveth and believeth in me shall never die" (III, ix).
Carton's need for real motivation to live and his wish to die have
been apparent from the beginning, but now they are fused and to be
fulfilled within the context made clear by the allusion. The "solemn
words" are most familiar perhaps in the service for the burial of the
dead, but they are first those of Christ in *St. John* (xi, 25), spoken
after Lazarus has been recalled to life; as the recall of Lazarus in the
Gospel anticipates the resurrection of Christ and the salvation of Man,
so the recall of Darnay through Carton's sacrificial death and the
rebirth of the spirit of Carton prefigure the redemption prophesied in
the final chapter.

The Christ-like image of Carton is now, though faint and uncertain,
inescapable, and—aware of the significance of the blood and wine
imagery—we look backward and forward seeking signs. The guilt of
Darnay is not really his own but, like Original Sin, that inherited
which he himself cannot remove and from the effects of which he must
be saved by one who, closely resembling him in his physical being,
will take upon himself through his own death the burden of guilt. The
guillotine has become for the people what the Cross was formerly: "It
was the sign of regeneration of the human race. It superseded the
Cross. Models of it were worn on the breasts from which the Cross was
discarded, and it was bowed down to and believed in where the Cross
was denied" (III, iv). But by his death Sydney Carton makes the
guillotine in reality what the people imagine it to be. Carton is clearly
the agent through whom good destroys evil. Motivated by love, he
undoes what Madame Defarge, who has been moved solely by hatred,
has wrought; finally, as she lies dead in Lucie's deserted apartment,
Madame Defarge has by all her efforts brought about only one fact, the
inevitable death of Sydney Carton, which has become to him psycho-
logically and spiritually necessary. Like one of the Fates, Madame
Defarge involves in her incessant knitting the symbols for individual
men, but of their death rather than their lives. She does not think;
nor does she feel outside of her one destructive motivation, and here
she might be said only to react: she becomes a further agent in the
series of evil causes and effects which she herself attributes to destiny.
At first it might appear that her antithesis is Lucie, who loves what

Madame Defarge hates, whose "weaving" with "the golden thread" of life (II, xxi) is in opposition to Madame's knitting, and whose Miss Pross, in fact, brings about the physical destruction of Madame Defarge. But her physical death is of no greater importance than that of Sydney Carton considered in itself. It is Carton himself who is her real antithesis. He rejects the one temptation to destroy her by force —when she gives him directions from the wine shop and her hand is on his arm—and destroys the corruption in her spirit and all its evil effects by allowing her to destroy him in the flesh. Where she is seemingly impersonal, he is obviously personal; where she controls herself and her surroundings, he apparently lacks control of either; where she is strong, he is weak. But it is Sydney Carton by his sacrifice, rather than Madame Defarge through her revolution, who shows the way to achieve that to which the French nation in its violence, or all mankind in fact, aspires.

But we must face the implications of the symbolism. Is there an equation to Christ in the person of Sydney Carton at the time of his sacrifice? Has Dickens put the story of Christ in a social and psychological context? I think not. The implication permeates the symbolic structure of *A Tale of Two Cities*, but the equation is never specific. Nor was it meant to be, for in the very inconclusiveness of Dickens's use of symbols—rather than in a contrived and ultimately meaningless allegory, which would leave the reader no room for the work of the imagination—lies the source of the effect of the work. In the case of Carton it is not an equation to Christ but the allusion to Christ which is significant. Acting in the image of Christ, Carton is, in his splendid sacrifice, the representative of the best achievement in Man. Darnay in his good faith with an old servant and in his love for his wife and child is the model of the more normal though less dramatic good in Man, as indeed the misguided French people themselves might become following their struggle for bread rather than death.

But these statements come dangerously close to meaning, and the meaning of the novel seen as a simple formula we know well enough. It is the method which is the source for power in *A Tale of Two Cities* —the suggestive yet inconclusive use of interacting images, upon which are built the reader's tensions, expectations, and imaginings.

A Tale of Two Cities

by Jack Lindsay

Charles Dickens was in a driven demoniac state of mind when the idea for *A Tale of Two Cities* came to him. The bracelet he sent to Ellen Lawless Ternan had fallen into the hands of his wife Kate; and he was determined to end his marriage and to seduce Ellen. But he was in the midst of the rehearsals which had finally brought himself and Ellen together; and he could not pause to think. Amid Kate's tears, Forster's disapproval and a generally unnerving situation, he carried on in his furious possessed fashion, determined to have his own way and yet to keep his hold on the public; and in the midst of this spiritually and physically racked condition, as he was holding back his agony of mind by acting and producing *The Frozen Deep,* the central idea of the novel burst upon him.

So much we know from his own statement. It is clear then that we should be able to find the imprint of his ordeal, his tormented choice, in the novel. One would expect writers on his work to concentrate on this problem; but so abysmally low is the standard of Dickens criticism that no one has even seriously raised the question at all.

I

Where then is the imprint of the situation to be traced? By solving this point we can begin to understand what the novel itself is about, and the part it plays in Dickens' development. One general aspect of the selection of theme is at once obvious. The deep nature of the breach he is making with all customary acceptances is driving him to make a comprehensive effort to grasp history in a new way. So far (except for *Barnaby Rudge*) he has been content to use certain symbols to define his sense of basic historical conflict and movement. Yet all the while the influence of Carlyle, both in his *French Revolu-*

"A Tale of Two Cities," *by Jack Lindsay. From* Life and Letters, *LXII (July–September, 1949), 191–204. Copyright © 1949 by Jack Lindsay. Reprinted by permission of the author. [This article appears in modified form as a part of Chapter XI of the author's book,* Charles Dickens *(London: Andrew Dakers, Ltd.; New York: Philosophical Library, 1950).]*

52

LINDSAY IS A DEVOTED MARXIST CRITIC THAT SHOULD BE BALANCED AGAINST ORWELL.

tion and his prophetic works like *Past and Present,* has been stirring him with the need for a direct statement of the historical issue as well as a symbolic one; and now, as he is coming close to a full confrontation of his opposition to all ruling Victorian values, he feels the need to set his story of conflicting wills in a manifestly revolutionary situation: that on which he had so long pondered as holding the clue to the crisis of his own world.

He had read and re-read Carlyle's history, till its theme and material were richly present in his mind; and now he wrote to the master asking for a loan of the cited authorities. The story goes that Carlyle jokingly sent him all his reference-books, "about two cartloads." And in the novel's preface Dickens wrote:

> It has been one of my hopes to add something to the popular and picturesque means of understanding that terrible time, though no one can hope to add anything to the philosophy of Mr. Carlyle's wonderful book.

But though this need to make a general reconsideration of the nature of historical movement and change was certainly central in the impulse that Dickens felt, he had to fuse the overt theme with a more immediately personal nexus of emotion and imagery before it could take full grip of him. In the midst of his domestic misery and frenzied play-acting he did not feel simply an intellectual need to revalue history. The desire to break through obstructions and to mate with Ellen could turn into the desire to write about the French Revolution only if some image or symbol made him feel a basic coincidence between his own experience and the Revolution. What then was this image?

It was that of the Imprisoned Man in the Bastille. The Lost Man who had been jailed so long that he has become an automaton of oppressed misery; who has forgotten even the source of his wrong, the cause of his dehumanizing misery; who needs to break out of the deadly darkness of stone in order to become human again, to learn the truth and regain love.

Here then is the core of the novel. The originally-intended title was *Recalled to Life.* Though Dickens dropped this for the whole novel, he kept it for the first part, and it expressed the originating emotion of the story. *A Tale of Two Cities* is built up from the episode of Dr. Manette's unjust imprisonment; and its whole working-out is concerned with the effects of that unjust deprivation of light and joy: effects which entangle everyone round the Doctor and recoil back on his own head in unpredictable ways. The Doctor's fate is thus for Dickens both a symbol of the Revolution, its deeds, causes, and consequences, and of himself, immured in a maddening cell of lies and cruelties, and seeking to break through into the truth, into a full and happy relationship with his fellows. It was the demented sense of environing pressures, of an unjust inescapable mechanism, which caught Dickens up in the midst of his wild mummery and gave him a sense of release when he determined to write the novel.[1]

It has been pointed out (by T. A. Jackson) that there is a close underlying similarity between the plot of *A Tale* and that of *Little Dorrit* (the preceding novel in which Dickens had at last fully marshalled his condemnation of Victorian society). Both Dorrit and Manette are imprisoned for a score of years; both are released by forces outside their control and then continue tormented by their jail-experience. Dorrit is haunted by fear of social exposure, which comes finally in the collapse of Merdle (the exposure of the theft basic in the economic system). Dorrit thus from one angle embodies Dickens's deep fears of the past, fears of being exposed, fears of being driven back on the terrible moment of loss which therefore threatens to return in exacerbated form. He also embodies the bad conscience of a whole society which dares not contemplate truly its origins. But in Manette the symbolism goes much deeper. The experience of oppressive misery has not merely twisted him, as it twisted Dorrit; it has broken down the whole system of memory in his psyche. The problem then is: What can restore consciousness? what can connect the upper and the hidden levels of the mind again? Manette is kept going by a blind exercise of the craft learned in the cell of oppression, and only the intrusion of events from the Revolution can bring him back to an active consciousness and release him from his obsession. But the drama of objectifying in action the pattern of memory, the repetition-compulsion which must be broken, inevitably brings its shocks, its apparent evocation of forces as destructive as those working from the traumatic level. The test lies in the way that evocation is faced, the way it works out. So Manette finds that the bitterness engendered by his sufferings as an innocent wronged man has tangled him up in a net (inside a larger reference of social action and reaction, guilt and innocence) from which escape is possible only after a great sacrifice has been made. The old must die for the new to be born; man cannot attain regeneration without accepting its sacrificial aspect. In the story this appears in the struggle between Darnay and Carton for Manette's daughter, and the solution that mates Darnay and the girl, yet sends Carton to a regeneration in death.

---

[1] We must not forget that from the 1790's the people had called Poor Houses *Bastilles,* and often burnt them down in a memory of the Bastille-attack. The use of the symbol here has therefore its links with Dickens's deep hatred of the Poor Law which he identified with his own child-fear of loss and rejection (especially in *Oliver Twist*).

In this dire tangle of moral consequences we see Dickens confront-
ing his own confused situation and trying to equate his own moment of
painful compelled choice with the revolutionary moment in which a
definite break is made with the old, amid violent birthpangs, and
makes possible the rebirth of life, the renewal of love and innocence.

The lacerated and divided state of Dickens's emotions at this moment of choice is revealed by the device of having two heroes who are
practically twins in appearance and who love the same girl. Both
Carton and Darnay are generous fellows, but one is morally well-
organized, the other is fecklessly a misfit. The latter, however, by his
devoted death reaches the same level of heroic generosity as his rival;
indeed goes higher. His gesture of renunciation completes the ravages
of the Revolution with its ruthless justice, and transforms them into
acts of purification and redemption, without which the life of renewed
love would not be possible.

Thus, in the story, Dickens gets the satisfaction of nobly giving up
the girl and yet mating with her. He splits himself in the moment of
choice, dies, and yet lives to marry the beloved, from whom the curse
born out of a tainted and divided society is at last removed. And at
the same time he is Manette, the man breaking out of a long prison-
misery, who seeks only truth and justice, and whose submerged
memory-drama projects itself as both the Carton-Darnay conflict and
the socially-impinging dilemma that disrupts and yet solves that conflict.

There are thus a number of ambivalences in the story; and Dickens
shows himself divided in his attitude to the Revolution itself. His
petty-bourgeois fear of mass-movements is still alive; but the fascination of such movements, which stirred so strongly in *Barnaby,* is even
keener than the fear. On the one hand he clings to the moral thesis to
defend the Revolution: the Old Regime was vilely cruel and bestialized
people, it could not but provoke excesses in return as the bonds
slipped. But this thesis, to which Carlyle had sought to give a grandiose
religious tang, now merges for Dickens with a deeper acceptance:

> Crush humanity out of shape once more under similar hammers
> and it will twist itself into the same tortured forms. Sow the same
> seed of rapacious license and oppression over again and it will surely
> yield the same fruit according to its kind.
>
> Six tumbrils roll along the streets. Change these back again to
> what they were, thou powerful enchanter Time, and they shall be
> seen to be the carriages of absolute monarchs, the equipages of feudal
> nobles, the toilets of flaring Jezebels, the churches that are not my
> Father's house but dens of thieves, the huts of millions of starving
> peasants.

This passage begins with the simple moral statement; but the tum-

brils, conjured up as mere counterpoises to the feudal carriages, become emblems of a great purification sweeping away the reign of the
old iniquity. They express a ruthless *transformation* of society and are
far more than an allegory of cruel tit-for-tat. Rather, they appear as
forces of triumphant righteousness.

Throughout the book there runs this ambivalent attitude to the
Revolution, shuddering, yet inclining to a deep and thorough acceptance. Not a blank-cheque acceptance, but one based on the subtle
dialectics of conflict revealed by the story of Manette. For that story,
symbolizing the whole crisis and defining its tensions in the depths of
the spirit, makes a serious effort to work out the process of change,
the rhythms of give-and-take, the involved struggles with their many
inversions and opposed refractions, the ultimate resolution in death
and love, in the renewal of life.

The working-out of the clash of forces is in fact more thoroughly
done than in any previous work of Dickens. The weakness lies in the
comparative thinness of characterization. The strain of grasping and
holding intact the complex skein of the story is too much for Dickens
at this difficult moment of growth. But his instinct is, as always, right.
He needed this strenuous effort to get outside himself: no other way
could he master the difficult moment and rebuild his foundations. After
it he could return to the attack on the contemporary world with a
new sureness, with new thews of drama, with new breadths of comprehension. The great works, *Great Expectations* and *Our Mutual
Friend,* were made possible. (I am not here dealing with those works;
but it is interesting to note that the imprisonment-theme finds its
completion in the contrasted and entangled themes of Miss Havisham
and the old convict, the self-imposed prison of the traumatic moment
and the socially-imposed prison of the criminal impulse, both merging
to express the compulsions of an acquisitive society.)

A Tale is not a successful work like the two novels that followed it,
but they would never have been written without it. An inner strain
appears in the rigidity of tension between the thematic structure and
the release of character-fantasy. Such persons as Manette, however,
show a new persistence of psychological analysis, and the Defarges
show what untapped sources of dramatic force Dickens could yet
draw on. The final falsification of the book's meaning came about
through the melodrama based on its material, in which the emphasis
put on Carton sentimentalized away all the profundities.

Lucie is meant to represent Ellen Ternan; but at this stage Dickens
knows very little about the real Ellen, and Lucie is therefore a stock-
heroine. Charles Darnay, the winning lover, has the revealing initials
Charles D. Dickens with his love of name-meanings can seldom resist
leaving at least one or two such daydream-admissions among the names

of a novel. Ellen was acting as Lucy in *The Frozen Deep* at the time when the novel's idea came.[2]

II

This analysis, drawing its method from a study of the way in which Dickens uses symbol and allegory in his novels, has enabled us to get under the surface, on which discussion has so far played. We can at least see roughly why the themes of *A Tale* burst out so magically in the midst of his personal crisis. What are those themes? The theme of the man released from a long deforming prison-experience into a new life, who carries against his will into the new life a repetition-compulsion from the past, and who thus has to discover as completion of his release the way of ending that compulsion. And the theme of the sacrificial death, which ends the compulsion and transforms violence into its opposite; which ends the whole vicious circle of the curse.

By noting the sources from which Dickens to a considerable extent drew these themes, we get important sidelights on to his creative intention. For Dickens was so closely entangled with certain currents of symbol-development in his day that we cannot get right inside his work unless we continually relate it to these currents of influences. So far the study of Dickens has been quite superficial and has neglected this aspect of his work.

In seeking the spiritual impacts behind any turn of development in Dickens it is always safe to look at Bulwer-Lytton's work; for that writer throughout his novels drew powerfully on certain traditional imagery, carried on from folk-days in various forms of popular or semi-popular expression. He influenced Dickens at decisive moments again and again: for example, his *Paul Clifford* led on to *Oliver Twist,* his *Night and Morning* led on to *Martin Chuzzlewit.* The work of his which underlay *A Tale of Two Cities* was *Zanoni* (1842).

Zanoni's method links closely with that of *A Tale.* Bulwer is openly writing a symbolic account of the creative process, in which all the characters, one way or another, represent phases or forms, types or anti-types, of the creator in his movement to enlarged or constricted life. This method is more rationalized in *A Tale,* but it is present in a degree that Dickens would scarcely have reached without knowing Bulwer's book. Further, *Zanoni* takes the French Revolution as its scene, to merge the personally creative struggle with a social convulsion of change.

Dickens revives his memory of *Zanoni* because he now feels the need

[2] In view of the deep and ceaseless fantasy of word-play in names in Dickens's work, it is no accident that *Manette* reversed is *Tenam,* not so unlike *Ternan.* Lucie Manette = Lucy (Ellen) Ternan.

to grapple with his pangs of consciousness in a related way. Inevitably he brings the method down to earth more than Bulwer, and to some extent changes the method of symbolic representations into one of dramatic realization. But the travail of his spirit appears in the extent to which the allegorical substratum intrudes and prevents a fully concrete character-projection.

Bulwer's attitude is far from that of Carlyle. With his odd kind of Tory anarchism he politically abhors the Revolution and tries consciously to reduce it to a demented terrorism. But in the working-out of his allegory he cannot help giving it further values, which in the end achieve something like a full acceptance of its action at deeper levels than those of intellectual judgment. For, if the Revolution is the moment when the creative process reaches its intensest moment of conflict and union (as *Zanoni* implies), then the schematic political attitude falls away and sets free a quite different conception, in which revolution and stability, death and life, are equally accepted as aspects of process.

Zanoni, the idealizing and integrating art-activity, is opposed to old Melnour, the contemplative and analytic mind. But both these figures are opposed in turn to Glyndon, emblem of art-science which strives to rise above convention and stereotype, but is stricken down by the attack of fear on the threshold of adventure into the unknown (the human future, the unconscious). Both Glyndon and Zanoni compete for possession of Viola (love, the affective life, union); and the spiritual drama of their struggles is linked throughout with the tumults and clashes of the Revolution. Bulwer, despite his hectic denunciations of the Terror, finds himself willynilly in the position of identifying the innermost struggle of human and artistic values with the struggle of basic social change.

His Viola is arrested in Paris at the height of the Terror (through the jealous hauntings of Nicot and Fillide). Glyndon, whose contact with her was the direct cause of her danger, has fled; but Zanoni steps in and substitutes himself for her on the guillotine.

The derivation of *A Tale* from *Zanoni* is certain; for it appears both in method and theme. But in the years between 1842 and 1859, Dickens's mind has transmuted *Zanoni's* tensions and forms into something very different. The frankly and wildly symbolic tale has been rationalized and psychologized, but the undissolved structure is visible. Dickens like Bulwer wants to define the crucial moment of personal pang and growth in terms of the revolutionary situation and to find by these means the clue to human and artistic growth. In Bulwer the emblem of new life is the Child, in Dickens it is the United Lovers. In Bulwer Zanoni must sacrifice himself to save the new life, because the idealizing activity has gone too far and has lost human sympathy;

and Glyndon must flee, because he is the artist who cannot break through his fear into a renewal of art and life. But the total effect of all the unions and cleavages, possessions and renunciations, is to liberate the creative image, to beget the child. Out of the revolutionary pangs of birth comes the continuity of life, the fresh stabilization of the life-process. Therefore Viola dies at the same moment as Zanoni sacrifices himself, and (as the book ends) the People come bursting with freedom into the prison, to find a dead mother and a helpless babe.

> Even in the riot of their joy, they drew back in astonishment and awe. Never had they seen life so beautiful; and as they crept nearer, and with noiseless feet, they saw that the lips breathed not, that the repose was of marble, and the beauty and the ecstasy were of death. They gathered round in silence; and lo, at her feet there was a young infant, who, wakened by their tread, looked at them steadfastly, and with its rosy fingers played with its dead mother's arms.

The terrible moment of creation is ended. There is only the in-breaking movement of union and freedom, which meets a new life apparently quite cut away from all parentage. But in the working-out of that new life the struggle will revive, the innocence will become tainted, the freedom will reveal its limitations and tensions, and the struggle of process will start all over again. But not at the same level. The decisive moment of death and renewal has given a fresh-start as well as reestablished continuity.

In *A Tale,* with its less obvious allegory, and its more direct acceptance of social process, the romantic formulas of lovers-restored-to-one-another and the defeated-curse are used, and it is the rejected or excluded one who makes the sacrifice. But however differently the ingredients are mixed, the kinship of pattern remains; and a consideration of *Zanoni* helps us much further to an understanding of the passionate moment when Dickens felt that at last he could and must use the French Revolution as material and setting for a novel.

III

It happens that we can go yet further and find the direct link between *Zanoni* and *A Tale,* the work which revived Dickens's memories of *Zanoni* at the time when he was moving near to his domestic collapse. This work is *The Dead Heart,* a play by a minor playwright and artist, Watts Phillips.

Watts Phillips had been trained by Cruikshank at the time when that artist was illustrating *Oliver Twist;* he studied in Paris and was present during the February Revolution of 1848, when, though his political understanding was slight, he felt much sympathy for the insurgents; he also knew Carlyle's *French Revolution* well. His play in part derived from an episode in Carlyle's book, which certainly lay also behind *A Tale.*

> I have a knowledge (from my long residence) of the French *people,* and know the literature of the revolution *well.* My only borrowing was from an incident related in Carlyle's history (concluding chapter of third volume) in which an old man, the Marquis de something, answers to the roll-call in place of his son (who is asleep) and takes *his place in the tumbril.*

But memories of 1848 certainly gave the vivifying touch. In letters from Paris during the upheavals Watts Phillips wrote:

> Glorious things are happening. Liberty *has* dawned on France. Hurrah . . .
> I came home last evening over the Pont Neuf, and stopped for some minutes to look at the crowd of buildings (the Cité) which formed the gloomy masses that stretched along the river's banks—the faint and flickering lights that shone on the dark waters—the tall towers of the various edifices, all so quiet and yet so grand in their indistinctness— when I was roughly disturbed in my meditations by crowds of fellows marching (from some banquet, I imagine) over the bridge and roaring the revolutionary songs. No sooner were they passed than a body of the Garde Mobile succeeded, their bayonets glistening in the moon- light.
> The *Ca ira* still ringing in my ears, I walked on, musing upon the scene, which might have been an extract from the drama of the First Republic; and when I looked up—standing in the old Place de la Révolution—I almost expected to see the tall, gaunt form of the guillotine, showing black against the sky, and blasting, like the upas with its hideous aspect, the passers by.

And at least once he seems to have been in some danger.

He composed *The Dead Heart* some three years before *A Tale,* though it was not produced till the year of the novel's publication, 1859. Boucicault had made an adaptation of Dumas's *Chevalier de la Maison Rouge,* in which the Bastille and the revolutionary crowd had appeared; and thus was the probable reason for the delay in staging Watts Phillips's play. In April, 1859, *A Tale* began its instalments, and Watts Phillips was at once dismayed:

> Of course they will make a play of Dickens's new tale, *The Two Cities,* and (if you have read it) you will see how the character of the man "dug out" of the Bastille will clash with the man in *The Dead Heart* written more than three years ago. . . . The tone of the resurrec- tion from the Bastille ought to have been *fresh* in my play, not in his story. It's very heart-breaking. (2 June.)

As a result, a speedy effort was made to produce the play, which was first acted on 10th November, 1859. Then the final instalments of the novel turned out to have used the same denouement as *The Dead Heart*—the substitution of one man for another at the guillotine in an act of self-sacrifice.

A single theme may be used accidentally by novelists or playwrights; but when two main themes coincide and entwine (the resurrection from the living-death of the Bastille and the sacrificial death), it seems more than likely that there is some direct contact. The death-substitution theme was certainly floating about. Dickens had *Zanoni* in mind, and something of the sort might have been suggested by Dumas's play. The motive had appeared also in a play *All for Her* by Palgrave Simpson and Merivale. It is the combination of this motive with that of return-to-life which is surprising.

And there seems little doubt that Dickens had heard or read *The Dead Heart* well before beginning *A Tale*. The biographer of Watts Phillips says:

> The author, indeed, went so far as to say that the piece was "seen by Dickens long ago." It seems that when he first sent the piece to [the manager] Webster, the latter took it down to Brighton, and there read it to two or three friends, one of whom was the novelist.

This statement was never contradicted; and we may therefore assume that Dickens knew the play and had been moved by its conception, which he revived in his own form to express the crisis of change he felt in breaking with Kate.

What exactly then did he get from *The Dead Heart* which he did not get from Carlyle and Bulwer? The name itself gives a first clue. The Bastille is in some sort the Dead Heart, which must break open with new life and love. And when we look at the play itself, we find that its hero Robert Landry is exactly the figure we require as the halfway-house between Zanoni and Manette-Darnay-Carton. He begins as a hopeful young artist, is horribly changed by the hell of twenty years' imprisonment, returns to life, becomes a resolved revolutionary leader, cannot resolve his love-problem, and finds release from his inner contradictions by a redeeming death of sacrificial substitution. Here we meet the implications I have discussed of the *Zanoni*-theme, brought to a level of more manifest unity and providing the basis for the new splitting-up that Dickens carries out. Landry is Manette, Darnay, and Carton all in one: the sufferer, the reborn, the accuser of social evil, the revolutionary leader, the rent lover, the hopelessly-divided romantic. Also, through the way in which for Watts Phillips, 1793 and 1848, are emotionally merged, we get the contemporary impact more obviously than in *A Tale*.

Through this play then we can underline the extent to which

Manette, Darnay, and Carton are all one person, Dickens. Here, as in *Zanoni,* the emphasis is on the giving-way of the old before the claims of the new. The revolutionary moment breaks open, the contradictions which it has been perpetuating against its own will are abruptly overcome, and only the new life remains. In *Zanoni* this theme was embodied in the symbol of the Babe. Here it comes out in the fact that Landry dies to restore to Catharine Duval her son: the play ends with Catharine embracing the son and learning the truth about Landry by looking through the window as he mounts the guillotine. (By a stage-device the prison-walls slid away and the guillotine appeared: thus the two aspects, death and renewal, were brought together.)

The romantic hero, at the end of his tether, gives way to the youth who regains his mother. The hero is barred away and must go to death. (Note that the lost wife-mother in the play chances to be a Kate.) Thus the *Zanoni*-theme is redefined in a more rationally-mature way, which is more assimilable to Dickens's own inner conflict. We see that the Manette-Darnay-Carton complex holds a father-son conflict, of the sort later to come out clearly in *Edwin Drood.* The romantic artist, perverted by suffering and yet turned into a strong revolutionary agent, finds his completion by making way for the young Baptiste. Dickens feels himself confronted by the younger generation, Wilkie Collins and Sala, who go easily into issues that are still baffling for him; and by the young girls, his daughters and their friends, and Ellen Ternan, who turn easily to the loves and laughters he has lost or never had. But he refuses to accept the *Zanoni*-solution, the Babe coming out of the cleft prison-stone or Baptiste finding his mother's bosom again in safety. He wants desperately to share in the new life. So he splits up the Zanoni-Landry figure, and gives to Manette the horror and rebirth, the rigid accusation and the revolutionary conscience, and to Darnay and Carton the entangled conflict of love. Then one half of him can lose, because the other half wins. Carton-Charles goes down and renounces, but Darnay-Dickens takes the girl and finds his place in society.

A Tale was dramatized, as Watts Phillips had feared, and the public saw the connection of the two stories:

> The plays caught on, and their resemblance to each other attracted universal attention, society divided itself unto two factions—the Celestites and Dickensites, the Websterites and Phillipsites. Then came accusations and recriminations as to coincidences and plagiarisms, and bad blood arose on both sides. (Coleman.) [3]

[3] See *Watts Phillips: Artist and Playwright,* by E. Watts Phillips (1891), written after *The Dead Heart* had been successfully revived by Irving. Phillips was an attractive person of considerable intelligence and a quick witty draughtsman's eye. There were many points of similarity between his outlook and Dickens's. He too

IV

An examination then of the inner movement of symbolism in *A Tale* and the relation of the symbolism to kindred contemporary trends makes sufficiently clear the potence of the image that burst on Dickens in the midst of his personal crisis. The examination reveals important subtleties that have been ignored or explained away in the general movement of falsification which has held appalling sway (except for the rare comments of a few critics such as Bernard Shaw and Edmund Wilson) in the realm of Dickens "criticism." *A Tale* is not a great work, though like almost anything written by Dickens it has great elements; but when it is seriously approached, it turns out to be a work of high interest, yielding some essential clues to the workings of Dickens's mind and of creative symbolism in general.

attacked the Victorian Sunday, loved Paris, wrote on a visit to the Morgue, respected French culture more than English-Victorian, and was fascinated by the London underworld. He wrote (1854–5) *The Wild Tribes of London,* describing the slum-folk.

Dickens and the Fiery Past:
A Tale of Two Cities Reconsidered

by G. Robert Stange

"But why waste time on Dickens when one can read Henry James?"
The sophisticated graduate student who asked the question did not
really want an answer; he wanted to provoke critical discussion. The
obvious reply is that life, thank God, is long enough to include both
these novelists, but the question's chief use is to define two permanent
poles of literary art. James, in his search for a flawless technique,
sustained control, and delicate effect, is worlds apart from the sprawl-
ing, uneven, essentially imperfect Dickens. In this respect, at least,
Dickens is like the "imperfect" Shakespeare; by dint of his extraordinary creative energy, the very scope of his art, he enters the rare cate-
gory of writers who have ceased to be detached objects of contemplation, and become instead parts of everyone's past.

Seen under the aspect of eternity Dickens may not be a greater
novelist than James, but he can speak more easily than James could to
many more people. James could not have afforded to be vulgar as
Dickens was; he could not have allowed himself the artistic errors that
Dickens continually falls into; he could never have cried over his
characters so unabashedly, nor laughed so uproariously. When we read
the great fictional craftsmen we are impressed by the justness with
which they have *rendered* a character or an aspect of life; we approve
them by considering that they have been faithful to our experience of
the world. But the characters of Dickens' novels have an independent
existence; his world operates by its own laws, and after being immersed
in it we return to our world with heightened perceptions and a finer
sense of reality. In reading Dickens one tends to compare the characters of real life with those in his novels: no one ever praised Grand-
father Smallweed or Mr. Micawber or Mrs. Gamp for being faithfully
rendered; we find instead human beings who resemble *them*.

There are many reasons why Dickens' novels are the best kind of thing for young people to read. On the most general level, his great creative energy, the easy extensiveness of his work, help suggest to the young the joyful possibilities of all art. His sensitivity to the beauty and interest of the humblest aspects of life, his vibrant sympathy, are fine examples of responses that must inform any permanently significant literature. A novel by Dickens should be in every high school curriculum. But I have sometimes wondered why that novel has almost invariably been *A Tale of Two Cities.* Reflection suggests an initial advantage in its being the shortest—next to *Hard Times*—of Dickens' fourteen novels. However, I think there are other more worthy reasons, and some of them are good.

This particular novel was most widely accepted as a high school assignment about half a century ago. At that time, we must assume, it reflected contemporary literary enthusiasms. In the 1890's Freeman Wills' play, *The Only Way,* an adaptation of Dickens' novel, was an enormous success. I suspect that, for this reason, our pedagogical forbears found *A Tale* the most immediately relevant, the most "modern" of all Dickens' novels.

The fact that this novel is unlike most of Dickens' work may also have recommended it to teachers. There are more big scenes in it than in any of his other novels; there is less of the grotesque, fewer episodes and characters that the inexperienced reader might consider quaint or antiquated; and there is, almost uniquely in Dickens, a single plot that is unravelled with speed and concision, and which always dominates both the characters and their *milieux.* The novel's relatively simple construction makes it easy for the reader to get into and through the story; it invites an immediate and simple response. In addition to these not inconsiderable advantages conscientious teachers must have regarded the historical background of the novel as a kind of unearned dividend that could be drawn on at need. If one could get a little history in by the back door, so much the better.

Some of these reasons have lost their force over the last thirty or forty years. There may be some point in reconsidering the exclusive assignment of this novel (if I were choosing for a high school course I should pick *Great Expectations* or *David Copperfield*), but I do not think we need regard *A Tale of Two Cities* as a really bad choice. It may be—along with *Hard Times*—the least Dickensian of the novels, but no novel of Dickens is uninteresting; none can fail to enchant or to instruct us. The very weaknesses of Dickens are illuminating, and if in this novel he has, as I believe, failed to achieve his ambitious plans, the novel nevertheless has qualities which make it uniquely valuable.

In considering the general scheme of *A Tale of Two Cities* we can discern three main points of departure from which the conception obviously develops. Dickens tells us in his preface that the main idea of the story came to him while he was performing in an amateur production of Wilkie Collins' play, *The Frozen Deep*. This melodrama, which was much admired by Dickens and his friends, is about two men, Antarctic explorers, who are in love with the same girl. One of the heroes (played by Dickens) sacrifices his life to save his rival's, and by this sacrifice is morally regenerated. Dickens' comment on the play helps emphasize the fact that in the novel Sydney Carton's sacrificial death, and more important, the whole theme of violent death and regeneration, must be regarded as the "main idea."

Though *A Tale* ends with Carton's execution, its beginning and middle are dominated by the sufferings of Doctor Manette, the Bastille prisoner. Dickens had considered calling the novel "Buried Alive," or "The Doctor of Beauvais," and the theme of imprisonment runs darkly through it, second in importance only to the theme of rebirth. During the years to which *A Tale of Two Cities* belongs Dickens seems to have been obsessed by the notion of a prisoner buried alive, suddenly released to the light of everyday life, and having to re-form his connections with free men, to learn again the meaning of love and responsibility. Both *Little Dorrit,* which preceded *A Tale,* and *Great Expectations,* which followed it, develop the prison theme; one works out the comic and tragic conditions of prison life itself, the other treats with pathos and searing irony the ideas of innocence and guilt in terms of the bond between the convict and the "free" and "guiltless" men who judge and sentence him. "Recalled to Life" is the title of the first book of *A Tale.* Doctor Manette's story is not developed with irony or complication, but the narrative of his experiences is as much an inciting motif of the novel as is the story of Sydney Carton. Both lives are broadly conceived in the pattern of suffering, death (either real or symbolic), and regeneration. Both private lives reflect and mesh with the great public events which, we are to see, follow the same pattern.

From Thomas Carlyle's *French Revolution,* originally published in 1837, Dickens derived the account of historical events within which he could dispose his private dramas. He was devoted to Carlyle's history, "the book of all others," according to his American friend, J. T. Fields, "which he read perpetually and of which he never tired—a book for inexhaustibleness to be placed before every other book." In 1850 Dickens wrote to his friend and biographer, John Forster, that he was reading *The French Revolution* "again, for the 500th time," and he concluded the preface to his novel with the statement that "no one can hope to add anything to the philosophy of Mr. Carlyle's wonderful book."

Many of the details of Dickens' novel are drawn directly from Carlyle. Certain great scenes, such as the storming of the Bastille or the operation of the guillotine, are as firmly based on Carlyle's history as are such smaller details as the firing of the chateaux or, even, the four valets who help Monseigneur to dress. But in emphasizing these specific obligations one may overlook the more fundamental debt. Dickens' choice of the historical event which would be the subject of his novel, the ideas about history and man's relation to it which shape his treatment of that subject, all derive from Carlyle.

As Carlyle saw it, history evolved through successive stages of destruction and reconstruction. The study of the past had not so much an intellectual as a moral purpose: every fact of life is a matter of divine revelation; by scanning history, the inspired writer finds the prophetic truth that would guide the future. Fundamental to Carlyle's views was the belief that each new age was born like the phoenix out of the ashes of the past. The men of his time were entering, he felt, an age of reconstruction and rebirth; the preceding age of Revolution he interpreted as the period of apocalyptic fire out of which the new world would rise. In his book he only implied his moral judgments of the French Revolution; in conversation he was more direct, and described it as "the suicidal explosion of an old wicked world, too wicked, false and impious for living longer." His book was planned to emphasize the dramatic—and symbolic—aspects of the historical event: its three sections are concerned with the *ancien régime,* the Terror, and the building of the new society.

Two attitudes that emerge from Carlyle's view of history are particularly important to Dickens' fiction. First, though Carlyle was disgusted by the theories and practice of the revolutionists, he was able to welcome their fury as a cleansing flame. He observed the noble and vicious events of the catastrophe with a grim, religious certainly, never moved by revolutionary ardour, but never doubting the necessity of revolutionary violence. And second, he did not entertain the conception of the past as a subject of study in its own right. We of the twentieth century are so imbued with the notion of a "scientific," "objective" study of history that we forget how recent an idea it is. For Carlyle the past lay like a scripture which, being interpreted, revealed the eternal and inexorable laws of sin, expiation, and redemption. That a past time might be dispassionately reconstructed, or that it might be interpreted, not by the standards and beliefs of the present, but by its own systems of order and value, never occurred to the historian Carlyle, nor to his disciple Charles Dickens.

Both the general approach and the structure of *A Tale of Two Cities* are shaped by Carlylean doctrines. Dickens chose the French Revolution as his subject because he, too, saw it as the event which ushered in the modern world. And then, his idea of the past led him to write historical fiction with a difference. By nature Dickens was contemptuous of the past: he had neither the patient enthusiasm of the antiquarian nor the curious eye of the scholar; he wished to regard history only from a moral (and preferably superior) standpoint. Consequently, we do not have in this novel the careful reconstruction of manners and morals which occasionally gives such richness to the novels of Scott or Thackeray. Dickens' reader is not made to feel that he has been projected into a bygone time. Instead, the novelist uses the condescending "in those days" formula; he continually reminds us that we have escaped from the trammels and superstitions of the past into a freer, better age: "But indeed, at that time, putting to death was a recipe much in vogue with all trades and professions, and not least of all with Tellson's." (Book II, Ch. 1.) Or we find him sneering at "dear old institutions," which turn out to be such things as the pillory, the whipping post, and blood money, all fragments of "ancestral wisdom, systematically leading to the most frightful mercenary crimes that could be committed under Heaven." (Book II, Ch. 2.)

Dickens, then, is encouraged by Carlyle's theory to regard the past primarily as a storehouse of lessons, a terrible moral drama. In constructing his novel—it seems clear—he conceived his problem as one of integrating the personal lives of his characters with the wider pattern of history. It is the principal scheme of the novel to show the individual fate mirroring and being mirrored by the fate of the social order. The lives of both Doctor Manette and Sydney Carton are, in a sense, parables of the Revolution, of social regeneration through suffering and sacrifice. The Doctor's return to life illustrates the stumbling course of the new order, released from its dark dungeon of oppression and misery, finding its place in a new and juster world. And Carton embodies both the novel's central narrative theme and its profoundest moral view: his past of sinful negligence parallels the past of eighteenth-century Europe; his noble death demonstrates the possibility of rebirth through love and expiation.

The web of moral interdependence is very closely spun. John Forster, who often echoed Dickens' own views, emphasized this aspect as the finest feature of the novel: "There is no piece of fiction known to me, in which the domestic life of a few simple private people is in such a manner knitted and interwoven with the outbreak of a terrible public event, that the one seems but part of the other." Indeed, in a work of serious historical interest it is necessary that the reader have a sense of his own connection with—even his own responsibility for—a social crisis. A modern example would be Ernest Hemingway's persuasive epigraph reminding the American or English reader that the knell that sounded the death of the Spanish Republic tolled also for him.

Dickens, in a similar manner, set himself the task of persuading his readers that they were not islands entire of themselves, but involved in the injustice that led to the Revolution and in the violence that it set loose. "The world," Dickens is reported to have said, "is so much smaller than we think it; we are all so connected by fate without knowing it; people supposed to be far apart are so constantly elbowing each other; and tomorrow bears so close a resemblance to nothing half so much as to yesterday."

This notion of reciprocity between private and public, England and France, past and present, imposes a pattern of parallelism on Dickens' novel. It had to be a tale of *two* cities, not just a story of revolutionary Paris. Every device that ingenuity suggested was used to connect the seemingly placid world of England with the upheaval in France. Symbolically the point is emphasized by the footsteps which echo on the quiet corner of Soho where Lucie lives with her husband and father. These echoes, becoming increasingly ominous, finally mingle with the "headlong and dangerous footsteps . . . raging in Saint Antoine afar off." (Book II, Ch. 21.) Mechanically considered, the novel is divided almost equally between the two countries: of the forty-five chapters, two recount the parallelism of events in England and France, nineteen are set in England, and twenty-four in France. The subject, however, did not permit a true balance of emphasis; all of Book III takes place in France, so that the movement of the novel is directed away from England toward the heart of the revolutionary strife.

In terms of action Dickens seems to have tried to establish a correspondence between the two nations, but not to have quite succeeded. Tellson's Bank is to some extent conceived as agent of the Old Order, and therefore as evidencing its guilt, but it turns out to be quite an attractive (perhaps because thoroughly English) place. The description of the London mob attacking the funeral procession of the Old Bailey spy (Book II, Ch. 14) must have been designed to balance the descriptions of French mob violence with a home-grown Fleet Street variety. But the episode seems irrelevant to the story, and is handled in an oddly perfunctory way, ending in a moralistic rather than a dramatic strain: ". . . the crowd gradually melted away, and perhaps the Guards came, and perhaps they never came, and this was the usual progress of a mob." Jerry Cruncher, the grave-robber, who for professional reasons joins the attack on the funeral, was probably conceived as an English counterpart to the implacable Defarge, but no significant parallel is established.

The process of doubling is observable in the treatment of the main characters. The shiftless Carton and the virtuous Charles Darnay are doubles. Darnay is tried as an enemy of the state both in England and

in France; in both cases he is unjustly accused, and in both is saved
by Carton. Darnay has an original French name, D'Evrémonde, a
coupling of the English word *every* and the French word *monde*. The
association is with *tout le monde,* suggesting that Darnay is an Anglo-
French Everyman. Lucie Manette, finally, is the child of an English
mother and a French father.

The difficulty in this attempt to yoke the worlds of London and
Paris by violence together is that Dickens had to forego his usual confident placing of English characters in English scenes. He was able to
make use of a number of Englishmen, but he had to violate both
fictional probability and historical possibility by transporting them all
to Paris in the Year of Terror, 1792. Then, the absence of English
backgrounds prevents, I think, the unhampered flowering of his comic
spirit. The comedy that appears in *A Tale* is only a faint echo of the
old Dickens. Mrs. Cruncher's "flopping" is purely verbal humor, and
attached to a pathetic situation. There are some deft satirical strokes
in the description of Darnay's first trial, and a droll description of the
fresco of Cupid in Tellson's Paris office, "still to be seen on the ceiling
in the coolest linen, aiming (as he very often does) at money from
morning to night." But these touches are few and comparatively weak.

Dickens' comic spirit was, I am sure, inhibited by the nature of his
material. Comedy is based on the familiar and the particular; the wide
gestures of intense passion or suffering are far removed from the minute turns of comic vexation. For this reason comedy would obviously
be inappropriate to a study of revolution. However, there is another
reason for the gravity of *A Tale of Two Cities:* Dickens' best comedy
is verbal; Mrs. Gamp (in *Martin Chuzzlewit*) is supremely comic because of the wild irrelevance of her speech, a speech which rises from
the carefully perceived cadences of the vulgar language. Since Dickens
rarely made good comedy out of the well-bred, it seems likely that in
this novel, where he was pretty much confined to upper middle-class
people, aristocrats, and foreigners, he was bereft of the native, collo-
quial speech upon which his genius fed. He was not up to creating
comic French characters and, indeed, for reasons of historical consistency, the Frenchmen had to be a grim crew.

In the absence of the comic spirit other means had to be used to
vivify the novel, so it is no surprise to find that Dickens spoke of
setting himself "the little task of making a *picturesque story,* rising in
every chapter, with characters true to nature, but whom the story
should express more than they should express themselves by dialogue."
It is one of the great weaknesses of the novel that Dickens attempted
to rely on plot rather than on character, but it is one of its strengths—
as well as its most distinctive feature—that it became a novel of *pic-*

tures. So marked is the painterly quality of *A Tale* that one's memory of it is dominated by a series of *tableaux vivants,* scenes without dialogue, but with a composition so clear that one tends to see them within the limits of a frame.

The most memorable scenes are charged with symbolism and become a primary means of shaping the reader's judgment of the Revolution. The first glimpse of France that the novel provides is the scene of the broken wine cask in Chapter Five. The two paragraphs in which this is contained are so purely visual that they might almost stand for the description of a painting called—let us say—"The Broken Cask." To this the novelist has added a notation of sound effects, "a shrill sound of laughter and amused voices," and a final sentence that sends the participants back to their usual tasks, and rounds out the scene. The great paragraph which describes the Carmagnole is another *tour de force* of word painting (Book III, Ch. 5), as is the picture of the men sharpening their bloody "hatchets, knives, bayonets, swords" at the grindstone (Book III, Ch. 2). These episodes are peculiarly interesting in that they are imagined to exist in the spatial dimensions of picture rather than in the temporal flow of narrative or verbal description. Dickens concludes his picture of the grindstone, for example, by saying: "All this was seen in a moment, as the vision of a drowning man, or of any human creature at any very great pass, could see a world if it were there." These three most elaborate pictures serve to create an intense emotional impression of the historical action of the novel. Each is a scene of passion and violence, each is presented with the clarity and overcharged feeling of a vision in delirium. This frenzy, Dickens would have us conclude, *is* the Revolution. It is through picture that he chose to control our responses: "It has been one of my hopes," so runs the preface, "to add something to the *popular and picturesque* means of understanding that terrible time, though no one can hope to add anything to the philosophy of Mr. Carlyle's wonderful book." (The italics are mine.)

Though there are no other pictures as highly wrought as these I have mentioned, the tableau technique is the ruling method of the book. Dickens tends throughout to make important episodes into set-pieces which are more visual than strictly dramatic. Since such passages are obviously separable from the surrounding matrix of narrative, the unity of tone in the novel suffers, but in his use of the stylized image Dickens developed a method that owes nothing either to the theatre (the source of much of his technique) or to the fiction of his predecessors and contemporaries. There is a groping toward a new form of the literary picturesque, the creation of an image which derives more from the conventions of painting than of literature, but which makes use in an impressionisic way of sound and movement. Dickens spoke justifiably of adding something to the "picturesque" means of understanding.

The general conception of *A Tale of Two Cities* is so grand that one is tempted to overlook the novel's technical faults. But faults there are, some of them unforgivable, many of them quite instructive. The elements of sentimentality and melodrama are no more persistent here than in some of the earlier novels, but as always, they are unpalatable to the modern reader. Lucie Manette's heart-rending reunion with the father she has never known is simply not prepared for:

> "And if, when I shall tell you of my name, and of my father who is living, and of my mother who is dead, you learn that I have to kneel to my honored father, and implore his pardon for having never for his sake striven all day and lain awake and wept all night, because the love of my poor mother hid his torture from me, weep for it, weep for it!" (Book I, Ch. 6.)

The illustrious analogue here is the reunion of Cordelia and Lear, but to define the differences between the two scenes is merely to become impatient with Dickens.

Similarly, Sydney Carton's declaration of love to Lucie is entirely possible, even noble, but it is undermined by sentimentality.

> "In my degradation, I have not been so degraded but that the sight of you with your father, and of this home made such a home by you, has stirred old shadows that I thought had died out of me.
>
> .   .   .
>
> "Will you let me believe, when I recall this day, that the last confidence of my life was reposed in your pure and innocent breast, and that it lies there alone, and will be shared by no one?" (Book II, Ch. 13.)

What is wrong in this passage is not so much the emotional situation, which we could be persuaded to believe in, as the language: there are too many dreams, and souls, and homes, and innocent breasts.

Some of Dickens' characteristic mannerisms grew all out of bounds in *A Tale*. Repetition was an endemic Victorian rhetorical device of which Dickens was always fond, but in no other novel is it so obtrusive. Observe the opening paragraph: "It was the best of times, it was the worst of times, it was the age of wisdom, it was the age of foolishness, it was the epoch of belief, it was the epoch . . . ," etc. Perhaps some of the repetitions and parallels were intended to emphasize the interconnections of twin realms of the novel, but too often the device becomes merely a trick. It does not add to the reader's experience to find the titles of chapters in balanced pairs, "The Fellow of Delicacy" followed by "The Fellow of No Delicacy," and "Knitting" followed by "Still Knitting." These verbal devices evidence a curious lack of control, a tendency to depend for effect on mere smartness.

One stylistic problem that Dickens did not quite overcome was the challenge of rendering the quality of foreign speech. Many novelists (and more dramatists) have been defeated in their efforts to make foreigners sound really foreign; on the whole Dickens has done pretty well. He was for the most part content to give the French dialogue a slightly stilted quality, the result usually of a literal translation of French idiom. M. Defarge's first statements are illustrative: " 'Say, then, my Gaspard, what do you do there?' . . . 'What now? Are you a subject for the mad-hospital?' " This, at least, sounds exotic without suggesting that the speaker has an imperfect grasp of his own language, but the method of rendering idioms literally can easily become absurd. One bit of dialogue runs, " 'One can depart, citizen?' 'One can depart,' " and French readers have been particularly annoyed by such solecisms as "the Bridge of the Pont-Neuf." However, clumsy as these locutions are, it is profitable—and to Dickens' advantage—to compare his efforts with Hemingway's valiant attempt to render the spirit of Spanish speech in *For Whom the Bell Tolls.* Hemingway's earthy Spaniards sound as queer as Dickens' Parisians.

But if there are weaknesses in Dickens' technique, there is also strength in many of the smaller touches which give richness to the novel. Much of the effect of *A Tale* is a result of artful patterns of imagery. The pervading image of the road, for example, runs through the whole book. The first chapter, which opens with a general description of the period, ends with a reference to the figurative road along which all men will be carried in the years ahead of them. The second chapter, which begins the narrative, makes the figure of speech literal: "It was the Dover road that lay, on a Friday night late in November. . . ." When, in the course of the novel, we encounter many roads upon which the characters drive or ride, none, thanks to the explicitness of the opening chapter, is without metaphorical significance.

Sometimes the imagery is allegorical. In the scene of the broken wine cask, which I have already mentioned, Dickens makes it obvious that the wine symbolizes blood, and the multiple meanings of wine and blood are then developed. Defarge's wineshop is the center of revolutionary action; we are led to reflect that the fellowship of blood and wine has many guises. Affecting the reader, however, on a more instinctual level are the images—which tend to run together—of fountains, flood, and fire. The fountain which is the center of the life of Saint Antoine becomes a symbol of the irrepressible force of humanity welling up against repression. After the wicked Monseigneur's carriage has run down a child, the novelist tells us, "The water of the fountain ran, the swift river ran, the day ran into

evening, so much life in the city ran into death according to rule . . .
all things ran their course." (Book II, Ch. 7.) The Saint Antoine
fountain has its rural counterparts: "The fountain in the village
flowed unseen and unheard, and the fountain at the chateau dropped
unseen and unheard—both melting away, like the minutes that were
falling from the spring of Time." In the passages that follow, the
water of the chateau fountain seems to turn to blood, and the village
fountain becomes the rallying place for the populace, the symbol of
their common humanity, of the force of life that cannot be put down.
In the chain of imagery the fountain images give way to a flood, a
sea, and the sea is succeeded by fire. The flowing water may be curbed
or checked, but it cannot be stopped, and it can soon turn from a
beneficent to a destructive force.

One of the powerful features of Dickens' art which should not go
unmentioned is his strong sense of the lusts and guilts and passions
which lie under the surface of human consciousness. It is notable
that his treatment of the Revolution is free of sentimental notions as
to the essential goodness of man. The Terror is conceived as both a
cleansing and polluting force, but men are shown to be attracted to
violence for its own sake. There is also a deal of deep psychological
understanding in the treatment of Charles Darnay's attraction by the
"Loadstone Rock" of the Revolution. And for us who live in a world
of concentration camps, of political betrayals, and inexplicable con-
fessions there is something almost prophetic in Dickens' analysis of the
prisoner's state of mind:

> Similarly, though with a subtle difference, a species of fervor or intoxica-
> tion, known, without a doubt, to have led some persons to brave the
> guillotine unnecessarily, and to die by it, was not mere boastfulness,
> but a wild infection of the wildly shaken public mind. In seasons of
> pestilence, some of us will have a secret attraction to the disease—a
> terrible passing inclination to die of it. (Book III, Ch. 6.)

This is not only brilliant psychology; it has turned out to be good
history. It is in its grasp of its subject that the power and brilliance
of this novel are finally seen to lie. The novel's chief weaknesses are
the results of its excessive artificiality: its construction constantly calls
attention to itself. But in reacting against these smaller details we must
not forget that Dickens' main intention was to present a view of, to
"add something" to our understanding of the French Revolution. And
the more I consider this novel as an interpretation of that event, the
more successful it seems to me. One may quarrel with this or that detail of documentation but the historical view, in its broad outlines, is a
sound one. Dickens suggested that "this terrible Revolution" was an
inevitable response to injustice, but he showed also how revolutionary

ardor produced its own forms of injustice. Carton, describing the Revolution as a dark phase in the development of modern history, saw "the evil of this time and of the previous time of which this is the natural birth, gradually making expiation for itself and wearing out." This view of history was temporarily out of fashion, but there is some evidence that historians are now returning to it. Experience of the revolutionary era of our own century has led more influential writers to see the French Revolution as the critical event of modern history, as a cataclysm whose effects are still with us.

A Tale of Two Cities is a profoundly thoughtful, if not a theoretical book. It is the sort of novel that should be enormously *usable* for young people and for their teachers. Its technical weaknesses are of a kind that can illustrate the nature and problems of fiction, but what is much more important, its conception can vivify for us the meanings of the past, can offer us a reading of history, humane and deep, by a great artistic intelligence.

The Style

by Taylor Stoehr

Dickens' style has a characteristic flavor. It is, as specialists sometimes say, Dickensian. The following analysis is not intended as a comprehensive study of his style, but is rather an attempt to isolate some outstanding features of it which seem to me to produce its characteristic flavor, especially (1) Dickens' use of detail as an active ingredient in setting and plot, (2) his use of rhetorical devices such as anaphora and metonymy to order and connect these details, and (3) the effect of such usages on Dickensian characterization and plotting. As the reader will see, particularly in the treatment of Dickens' principle of ordering, I am not so much concerned with any single instance of his use of detail or rhetoric as I am with the general nature of these elements; consequently, terms like "anaphora" and "metonymy" should be interpreted very broadly in this context, as designating tendencies of method in Dickens' work rather than specific tricks in his bag of artistic expedients.

Because I want to ground my study in close analysis of stylistic features and their inner consistency and integrity, I concentrate here on a single novel. In later chapters, as the argument progresses, there will be more and more reference to other novels, but in the beginning *A Tale of Two Cities* must serve as a representative text. The *Tale* will be familiar to almost any reader I can expect to reach, including those who are not specialists in the field; yet it is a novel which, unlike most of the major works in the Dickens canon, has not received the critical attention it deserves from our generation. The *Tale* provides familiar material about which readers are likely to have fewer critical preconceptions than they have about other Dickens novels—an obvious advantage in presenting a new reading of an old master.

A Tale of Two Cities has sometimes been thought atypical of Dickens; if this were true, of course, it would not be suitable for the kind of representative analysis offered here. In some ways the *Tale* is special and unusual, but its peculiarities do not prejudice the case any more than the specialness of *Bleak House* or *Great Expectations* would. Each of Dickens' novels differs from its predecessors and sequels, because Dickens was a serious artist, who learned something from each book he wrote. Yet always much persisted of his style and manner, and it is what persists that we think of as Dickensian, the essence of his art. *Pickwick, Oliver Twist, Martin Chuzzlewit, David Copperfield, Hard Times, Little Dorrit*—it is hard to name a novel that does not seem unrepresentative of the canon in one respect or another, and yet they are all quite Dickensian too. In *A Tale of Two Cities* Dickens is perhaps at his most rhetorical; but he is always a highly rhetorical writer, and the heightening that may be seen in the *Tale* is not un-Dickensian so much as it is ultra-Dickensian. For stylistic analysis, this has not seemed to me a drawback but rather an advantage.

Unnecessary Detail

Like other novelists, Dickens has his stylistic ups and downs, his moments of brilliance and his lapses into self-parody. In his best writing and in his worst, the habits that constitute his style persist, and here as in the work of other great stylists these habits call attention to themselves, regardless of the success or failure of particular passages. Nevertheless, the passages of greatest excellence—what in poetry used to be called the "beauties"—deserve our closest attention, for we are interested in Dickens' style, after all, only because it is so often brilliant.

Dickens lovers and scholars have always been disposed to praise those parts of *A Tale of Two Cities* in which the revolutionary scene predominates—the Wine-Shop chapter, the murder of the Marquis, the storming of the Bastille—so it seems natural to begin with these. Nothing is more typical than the way the Wine-Shop chapter opens:

> A large cask of wine had been dropped and broken, in the street. The accident had happened in getting it out of a cart; the cask had tumbled out with a run, the hoops had burst, and it lay on the stones just outside the door of the wine-shop, shattered like a walnut-shell.

The beginning of interest lies in the concrete object, the thing; Dickens sets the scene, almost cinematically, by focusing on such particulars. Here the effect is that of a high-angle view, centered on the splintered cask, slowly moving down on the square. As we are brought closer, description slides into narration, still determined by the objects in the setting:

> All the people within reach had suspended their business, or their idleness, to run to the spot and drink the wine. The rough, irregular

stones of the street, pointing every way, and designed, one might have thought, expressly to lame all living creatures that approached them, had dammed it into little pools; these were surrounded, each by its own jostling group or crowd, according to its size.

Everything "run[s] to the spot"; people are mere adjuncts of the stones and wine. It is the scene that sticks in the memory. Places, buildings, all kinds of physical objects take up most of the available space in the Dickensian world. Later, when the revolutionary characters are introduced and made to come alive in their dazzling way, we discover that even in the delineation of character Dickens depends on the physical setting, the *mise-en-scène*, the concrete object, for his favorite effects. In the passage quoted it is the objects that have character, that exist "expressly to lame all living creatures that approached them"; in other passages the people derive much of their special kind of life from the things which invariably accompany them: Madame Defarge and her knitting, Doctor Manette and his cobbler's bench, Jerry Cruncher and his spiky hair, Gaspard and his nightcap are typical examples. This insistence on the bits and pieces of physical reality has attracted the attention of most of Dickens' readers in one way or another. George Orwell, perhaps the most interesting of the critics who discuss the problem, has even suggested that the abundance of "unnecessary detail" is "the outstanding, unmistakable mark of Dickens's writing." Orwell likens such details to "florid little squiggle[s] on the edge of the paper"—and he includes among them not merely physical objects given in the setting, but also bits of narrative, scraps of dialogue, all the trivia of plot and character. "Everything is piled up and up, detail on detail, embroidery on embroidery," and the result, concludes Orwell, is like a wedding cake, as much beyond criticism as the rococo—"either you like it or you do not like it."

The notion that the details in Dickens are "unnecessary" is not as simple as it sounds, for Orwell does not mean that the "little squiggles" do not function in the work; otherwise he would not have said that "it is by just these details that the special Dickens atmosphere is created." But exactly how do the details operate in the total impression? In what way are they both necessary and unnecessary? . . . That the details in Dickens are unnecessary from a certain point of view does not mean that they fail to contribute to the total effect. Indeed, from another point of view they *are* the effect. (Similarly, Victorian society might be usefully contemplated as merely the embodiment of that taste for objects and things which, as we say, characterized it.) Thus is the apparently superfluous detail indispensable simply by virtue of being a prominent part of the whole.

One can go further than this, however, in specifying the function of detail in Dickens' novels. He himself gives something of his views on the use of setting and props in a letter of advice written to a would-be contributor to his magazine:

> Suppose yourself telling that affecting incident in a letter to a friend. Wouldn't you describe how you went through the life and stir of the streets and roads to the sick-room? Wouldn't you say what kind of a room it was, what the time of day it was, whether it was sunlight, starlight, or moonlight? Wouldn't you have a strong impression on your mind of how you were received, when you first met the look of the dying man, what strange contrasts were about you and struck you? I don't want you, in a novel, to present *yourself* to tell such things, but I want the things to be there.

Such injunctions might come from any writer of fiction, but Dickens' suggestions are particularly interesting because they so very exactly describe his narrative method in the Wine-Shop passages. He begins with the larger situation, given in concrete detail yet suggesting the whole framing context. He moves next to some unit already mentioned in the description of the larger context (the sickroom, the sharp stones). Finally characters are introduced, in some close relation to the objects. The emphasis throughout is on things, not so much things that happen, that can be recounted (though they are important too, obviously enough), as things that are *there,* in the novel and in the novel's world. Once the scene has become a human one, the narrative continues to be organized around the bits and pieces of the physical context:

> Some men kneeled down, made scoops of their two hands joined, and sipped, or tried to help women, who bent over their shoulders, to sip, before the wine had all run out between their fingers. Others, men and women, dipped in the puddles with little mugs of mutilated earthenware, or even with handkerchiefs from women's heads, which were squeezed dry into infant's mouths; others made small mud embankments, to stem the wine as it ran; others, directed by lookers-on up at high windows, darted here and there, to cut off little streams of wine that started away in new directions; others devoted themselves to the sodden and lee-dyed pieces of the cask, licking, and even champing the moister wine-rotted fragments with eager relish.

Here, as in the passages already quoted, the details of the setting seem to determine the movement of the narrator's eye: the wine is sipped and dipped, squeezed out and dammed up and cut off; mugs and handkerchiefs, mud and fragments of wood, figure more prominently than the people handling them. Even the dramatic feeling—the passion and despair of the characters, the meanness of their daily lives—is given through these vulgar objects and their uses.

It is worth pressing this point, for by just such means do we feel the pressure of atmosphere which is so powerful in Dickens, the impression that the world is thick with moods and presences, that will affect the course of events and drive the characters to their fate. The "unnecessary details" and "needless ramifications" fill up this world, and whether needless or not they constrain and determine action as the pebbles of a gravelly soil at once guide and hinder the searching roots.

Furthermore, Dickens only seems to pack his world full to bursting with the merely incidental and fortuitous; more often than not the apparently needless and accidental details form part of a meticulous weaving which, as the novel progresses, leaves less and less to chance. Consider the following passage, which occurs after all the wine has disappeared from the street:

> The man who had left his saw sticking in the firewood he was cutting, set it in motion again; the woman who had left on a door-step the little pot of hot ashes, at which she had been trying to soften the pain in her own starved fingers and toes, or in those of her child, returned to it; men with bare arms, matted locks, and cadaverous faces, who had emerged into the winter light from cellars, moved away, to descend again; and a gloom gathered on the scene that appeared more natural to it than sunshine.
>
> The wine was red wine, and had stained the ground of the narrow street in the suburb of Saint Antoine, in Paris, where it was spilled. It had stained many hands, too, and many faces, and many naked feet, and many wooden shoes. The hands of the man who sawed the wood, left red marks on the billets; and the forehead of the woman who nursed her baby, was stained with the stain of the old rag she wound about her head again. Those who had been greedy with the staves of the cask, had acquired a tigerish smear about the mouth; and one tall joker so besmirched, his head more out of a long squalid bag of a night-cap than in it, scrawled upon a wall with his finger dipped in muddy wine-lees— BLOOD.
>
> The time was to come, when that wine too would be spilled on the street-stones, and when the stain of it would be red upon many there.

When one first comes upon it in the novel, this passage foreshadows little more than the explicit prophecy of the last sentence, but as we read further we find that the little details thrown out so lavishly, and as it were so casually, have their echoes throughout the story. We meet the same woodsawyer again, and we begin to connect him with the "Woodman Fate" of the opening chapter. We see and hear the stained feet again—the echoing footsteps in Lucie's life, the dancing feet of the Carmagnole, the cruel foot of Madame Defarge as she steadies the governor's head for her knife. The "tigerish smear about the mouth" is our first introduction to the "life-thirsting, cannibal-looking, bloody-minded juryman, the Jacques Three of St. Antoine." The tall citizen in the night cap is Gaspard, who has in him still another note, also to be "scrawled," after the murder of the Marquis: *"Drive him fast to his tomb. This, from* JACQUES.*"*

The whole narrative is webbed with such interconnections, based always on the foreshadowing or echoing detail. Such repetitions have the obvious function of promoting the unity and probability of the novels, but an even more important result is the creation of a density of atmosphere beyond the power of mere verisimilitude or circumstantiality to achieve: we are presented with a cosmos everywhere interdependent, so that even objects in the landscape contribute to the sense of an interlocking system. With their multiple linkages, the "unnecessary detail" and "needless ramifications" of Dickens' style and plot provide the very fiber and fabric of his tightly knit world. The notorious coincidences of his novels are not the weak expedients of melodrama, but have behind them this same cosmic rationale. Thus Dickens' friend and biographer John Forster reports:

> On the coincidences, resemblances, and surprises of life, Dickens liked especially to dwell, and few things moved his fancy so pleasantly. The world, he would say, was so much smaller than we thought it; we were all so connected by fate without knowing it; people supposed to be far apart were so constantly elbowing each other; and to-morrow bore so close a resemblance to nothing half so much as to yesterday.

Again and again, Dickens' stories depend on the "unnecessary," coincidentally related details of this small world . . . In the typical Dickens novel, then, the concrete detail not only gives a framework for the movement of the narrative (as in the Wine-Shop passages) and a medium for the establishment of unity and coherence in the total action of the plot (by means of foreshadowing and other devices based on repetition), but also creates, in its very abundance and multiplication, the characteristic Dickensian atmosphere, a world in which all seemingly trivial, unrelated objects, people, and events finally mesh in an intricate and self-contained pattern.

The Principle of Ordering

Dickens' extravagant fondness for enumerating the flotsam and jetsam of life (one way of viewing the needlessness of the detail) is combined with a similarly extravagant passion for order (so that the details must be made necessary). Every new impulse to expand and amplify is accompanied by a corresponding desire to curb and control. Thus generalized, of course, the paradox is recognized as a central fact of all art, and we must look further in order to discover anything of special relevance to our understanding of Dickens. We must consider the particular character of Dickens' materials, how he chooses them, orders them, and so forth; and this in turn will lead us into questions about Dickens' vision of the world and the choices it offers to any man.

Let us approach the problem in terms of *A Tale of Two Cities* itself. As is his usual practice, Dickens begins by mystifying us. We are rushing along the Dover Road, in the dead of night, to what distant event we know not. Later we discover the purpose of that journey, but for each solution to a mystery some new and even more tangled puzzle is introduced. Why was Doctor Manette imprisoned? Who is Charles Darnay? Why is Doctor Manette so disturbed by him? Whose are the footsteps that echo in Lucie's chamber? What did Defarge find in his search of 105 North Tower? By the end of the novel every question has been answered, but meanwhile the world presented to us is a rather strange one. It is not so much mysterious, even, as it is peculiarly discontinuous. We are offered, to be sure, a sequence of events: one thing leads to another, time passes, the ground goes by under foot. But there seems to lurk behind the façade of normal occurrences some secret meaning, every now and then intruding itself as though in warning of imminent catastrophe. These intrusions are woven into the pattern of ongoing events in such a way that the train is never broken, but they strike us differently, as isolated bits of another story somehow underlying the one that takes up the actual time and space of the narrative. The denouement consists of the discovery that these apparently disconnected elements are in fact related, and even form a logical sequence—the true action of the story that we have been reading. . . .

. . . In Dickens, both . . . insistent circumstantiality and the larger, subtler pressure of fate may be discerned, but neither is a mark of his style. The essence of his style is not found in the kinds of details, or the general direction in which they seem to lead, but in the principle that governs their disposition in particular sentences and paragraphs. To see what this principle is and how it works, let us return to the Wine-Shop chapter; Dickens is describing Saint Antoine and its citizens, who have now lapped up all they can of the spilled wine:

> The children had ancient faces and grave voices; and upon them, and upon the grown faces, and ploughed into every furrow of age and coming up afresh, was the sign, *Hunger*. It was prevalent everywhere. *Hunger* was pushed out of the tall houses, in the wretched clothing that hung upon poles and lines; *Hunger* was patched into them with straw and rag and wood and paper; *Hunger* was repeated in every fragment of the small modicum of firewood that the man sawed off; *Hunger* stared down from the smokeless chimneys, and started up from the filthy street that had no offal, among its refuse, of anything to eat. *Hunger* was the inscription on the baker's shelves, written in every small loaf of his scanty stock of bad bread; at the sausage-shop, in every dead-dog preparation that was

offered for sale. *Hunger* rattled its dry bones among the roasting chestnuts in the turned cylinder; *Hunger* was shred into atomies in every farthing porringer of husky chips of potato, fried with some reluctant drops of oil. [my italics]

There is much that will bear analysis in this passage, but for our present purposes what is interesting is the articulation of the narrative and descriptive materials by the use of the rhetorical device of *anaphora,* the repetition of the key word "Hunger" to introduce and mark off the successive items of the presented scene. This device, which may be seen at work very frequently in Dickens—for instance, in the Wine-Shop passages already quoted—epitomizes Dickens' method of ordering his imagined world. The details of the scene are not merely piled up, one upon another; rather, there is a kind of logic in their arrangement. Everything here is mentioned because it is a concomitant of hunger, because it is a familiar result or cause or symptom or contingency of that condition. Observation and report are controlled, selection is determined, by the key word. One cannot, however, argue the converse, that what is given in the scene necessitates the choice of the word "Hunger," for it is the word which tells the reader what to notice, how to take the descriptive elements. Substitution of another word— say, "Poverty" or "Misery"—would result in a different set of meanings for the same reported observations. Thus the principle of *relevance* in the passage seems to be determined by the choice of the anaphoric expression. But the principle of *order* in the passage seems to be differently derived. The reader is presented with a cinematic rendering of continuous space in continuous time, the narrator functioning as a camera-eye; details make their appearance according to their position in the imagined scene, one thing next to another, and still another next to that. We are invited to attend to the houses, to the clotheslines stretched from their windows, to the man sawing firewood in front of the houses, to the chimneys which show no sign of wood being burned inside, and back again to the street and its shops and shop signs, its chestnut stand, costermongers and their wares. Although the selection of details is determined by the anaphora, the ordering seems to be given by the scene itself, by the mere contiguity of things. Of course, one can discover other principles of order here—for instance, the gradual movement of the attention toward what little food there is— but the description is handled in such a way that these other principles of arrangement seem to be mere corollaries of the physical arrangement of the actual scene, as if one could not avoid seeing things in this order. Indeed, the camera-eye effect, the rendering of continuous space in continuous time, seems to imply a strict necessity to report everything just as it is; and if Dickens actually had been under such a necessity, there could be no order at all except the "natural" order of the observed scene. Such is, in fact, the impression one often gets in reading his descriptions. He manages this effect, without seeming to wander aimlessly and endlessly over the scene, by means of the same rhetorical device that allows him to exercise selectivity. The obligation to record everything is avoided by the use of anaphora, which acts as a delimiting device, a kind of lens and shutter marking off selected bits of the scene, moving the reader's attention from representative sample to representative sample, and thus building an impression of the whole from the enumerated parts. The rhetoric controls the time and space of perception and report by opening (and, at each new opening, also thereby closing) the windows of the linguistic medium, our access to the author's world.

Anaphora, then, seems to give Dickens his means both of exercising selectivity and of presenting a scene as if he were exercising no selectivity at all, as if he were merely reporting what is there to be seen, without any authorial influence or distortion. Clearly enough, this is not a use of rhetoric merely for its own sake. The flavor of the passage is not rhetorical at all; what one notices is the vehemence of gaze which so impressed Taine:

> The imagination of Dickens is like that of monomaniacs. To plunge oneself into an idea, to be absorbed by it, to see nothing else, to repeat it under a hundred forms, to enlarge it, to carry it, thus enlarged, to the eye of the spectator, to dazzle and overwhelm him with it, to stamp it upon him so firmly and deeply that he can never again tear it from his memory,—these are the great features of this imagination and style.

The cumulative process by which the word-idea *Hunger* becomes a distinctive figure against the background of the street scene, a whole to which all the parts contribute and cling, is analogous to the mechanism of visual perception: a series of ocular fixations (with corresponding eye-movements) is essential to the perception of even the simplest figure, and, within limits, the vividness of the image depends on the number as well as the "intensity" of fixations and movements. In the passage from the Wine-Shop chapter the vividness of the description may be partially accounted for by the anaphoric construction, each repetition of the word "Hunger" acting as a signal for "fixation" on that part of the whole which follows it. . . .

. . . Two kinds of order may be seen at work [in the Wine-Shop passage —ED.]—the order by juxtaposition given in the details themselves, and the directionless order superimposed by the anaphora. Contiguity determines both arrangements: on the one hand, the movement from detail to detail; on the other, the schematizing repetition and emphasis of the rhetorical frame. The details attract the eye and provide the continuity of a contiguous world. The anaphora marks off these details, or groups of them, one by one, drawing attention to the juxtaposition; but here the effect is not so much an emphasis on continuity as it is the opposite, a sort of discontinuity—a rhetorical net in which the details are caught in motion, like the arrested activity of a snapshot. Because the anaphora is neutral, in that it suggests no *particular* progression in the elements it frames, and yet at the same time does very strictly impose *some* order, the whole scene is thrown into a kind of relief. To borrow another cinematic concept, the effect is like that of a montage-cluster, a series of detail shots juxtaposed in time, as for example in the Odessa Steps sequence in *Potemkin*—or, perhaps even closer to Dickens' montage, the collocation of stills-in-sequence which Barnaby Conrad edited for his remarkable "movie," *The Death of Manolete* (others have borrowed the technique, as viewers of American television commercials can testify). In such models, it almost seems as if one thing does not lead to another; everything exists at once, juxtaposed, superimposed, articulated in the consciousness by the anaphoric pattern. The details are both isolated from and joined to each other by the rhetorical boundaries. The isolation in time and space—the caught moment—exactly identifies the photographic realism that is characteristic of Dickens' treatment of detail. Similarly, it is the articulation, the juxtaposition, the superimposition of such details that gives, by its combination of order and disjunction, the strangely unreal effect which we also associate with Dickens, the sense of a world all in pieces, where every fragment is nonetheless intimately and mysteriously involved with every other fragment.

Metonymies of Character and Plot

Sometimes the "montage-clusters" of details which Dickens invents seem to take particularly strong hold on his mind, and he repeats them, or parts of them, in other contexts. Anaphora and other schematizing devices can have the effect of freezing the separate units together in the memory as an associational whole, and thus provide the basis for still another metonymic principle of connection between the larger parts of a novel. For example, Kenneth Burke has explained how any part of such an "associational cluster" may do synecdochic duty for the whole:

And as regards our speculations upon the nature of "clusters" or "equations," would it not follow that if there are, let us say, seven ingredients composing a cluster, any one of them could be treated as "representing" the rest? In this way such an image as a "house" in a poem can become a "house plus," serving as proxy for the other ingredients that cluster about it (e.g., for the beloved that lives in the house, and is thus "identified" with it). Usually, several of these other ingredients will appear surrounding the one temporarily featured.

The cluster of details that forms the basis of a structural synecdoche like this may derive its original cohesiveness in several ways. Positional contiguity—the fact that the elements first occur in close proximity to each other, often strongly marked by anaphoric devices—may determine the connection. Then again, the pattern need not be set up in a single paragraph or even a single chapter. Take the example of the Stone Face cluster in *A Tale of Two Cities*: throughout several chapters of Book 2 various ingredients are associated through their connection (again, by contiguity) with the Marquis St. Evrémonde's face. The Marquis is introduced in Chapter VII of the second book:

> He was a man of about sixty, handsomely dressed, haughty in manner, and with a face like a fine mask. A face of a transparent paleness; every feature in it clearly defined; one set expression on it. The nose, beautifully formed otherwise, was very slightly pinched at the top of each nostril. In these two compressions, or dints, the only little change that the face ever showed, resided. They persisted in changing colour sometimes, and they would be occasionally dilated and contracted by something like a faint pulsation; then, they gave a look of treachery, and cruelty, to the whole countenance.

In the same chapter, after running down a child with his coach, the Marquis betrays his anger through this physiognomical peculiarity:

> "You dogs!" said the Marquis, but smoothly, and with an unchanged front, except as to the spots on his nose: "I would ride over any of you very willingly, and exterminate you from the earth."

Chapter IX begins with a description of the Marquis' château, and introduces the image of the stone face:

> It was a heavy mass of building, that château of Monsieur the Marquis, with a large stone court-yard before it, and two stone sweeps of staircase meeting in a stone terrace before the principal door. A stony business altogether, with heavy stone balustrades, and stone urns, and stone flowers, and stone faces of men, and stone heads of lions, in all directions. As if the Gorgon's head had surveyed it, when it was finished, two centuries ago.
>
> The great door clanged behind him, and Monsieur the Marquis crossed a hall grim with certain old boar-spears, swords, and knives of the chase; grimmer with certain heavy riding-rods and riding-whips, of which many a peasant, gone to his benefactor Death, had felt the weight when his lord was angry.

Later in the chapter, the Marquis' face begins its transformation to stone:

> Every fine straight line in the clear whiteness of his face, was cruelly, craftily, and closely compressed, while he stood looking quietly at his nephew, with his snuff-box in his hand.

In the Marquis we have a perfect model, almost a prototype, for the well-known Dickens caricature, complete with social mask, hidden motives, and an exaggerated oddity—the nose—which provides the necessary key to the connection between the apparent and the real character. The cluster of information about the Marquis—his cold indifference (to the child's death), his heritage of cruelty (the riding-whips), his crafty hatred (of Darnay, his nephew)—circles persistently about the central image of his masklike face with its pinched and dinted nose. Everything comes back to that mask, that nose, and those dints, which finally take on more life than the Marquis himself. . . .

As Burke points out, there is a special advantage to these circling yet fixed patterns of association, in that a single part of any cluster may be used synecdochically to suggest the whole. Typically in Dickens there is some pivotal detail that serves in this way; the image of the stone mask with its pinched nose sets off the train of associations. Thus at the end of Chapter IX, where Dickens sums up all the Marquis' sins and their punishment, he returns to this dominant image:

> The Gorgon had surveyed the building again in the night, and had added the one stone face wanting; the stone face for which it had waited through about two hundred years.
> It lay back on the pillow of Monsieur the Marquis. It was like a fine mask, suddenly startled, made angry, and petrified.

The mask has usurped the field; nothing else of the cluster remains. The Marquis has been totally dehumanized, and exists only as a stone face. Taine has pointed out this dehumanizing effect of Dickens' carica-ture:

> The tenacity of your imagination, the vehemence and fixity with which you [that is, Dickens] impress your thought into the detail you wish to grasp, limit your knowledge, arrest you in a single feature, prevent you from reaching all the parts of a soul, and from sounding its depths.

But Taine short-changes Dickens' genius. This static, almost staring effect in the characterization of the Marquis, the fascination with his nose, accounts for the vividness of the characterization, just as the repetitive, "fixing" devices such as anaphora account for the vividness of the scenes. Actually Taine's complaint has to do with the lack of conventional realism in Dickens—we do not see "all the parts of a soul," the contradictory motives, the paradoxes of behavior that give an illusion of depth. But Dickens' verisimilitude is of another sort: the static quality is necessary to the photographic precision and clarity, while the third dimension—apparent depth—is given in the *meaning* of the character, by the use of associational clusters circling round a central image.

Dickens' iconography is in no sense unsophisticated or unpsychological. In the example of the Marquis' nose, the Marquis' defining quality is not ordinary anger but rage, habitually suppressed and therefore white-hot. In the stone mask with the pinched, pulsating dints in the nose, Dickens manages to express both the fury and its suppression. Moreover, while the Marquis' nose gives us the key to his character, other elements in the scene itself are used to elaborate this indirct presentation. When the Marquis leaves the town house of Monseigneur, furious because he is out of favor, the anger is allowed to show only in his pulsating nose. But for once the image is not adequate to the power of the feeling, which is actually expressed in the scene that follows, when the Marquis' *coach* runs down a helpless child—thus conveying, by a perfectly appropriate metonymy, the murderous rage that possesses him. In general, the Marquis cannot be allowed to have any direct contact with the fulfillment of his fiery desires, since it is his character to suppress his feelings. His ancestors wielded the riding whips, his coach acts out his fury, his nose betrays his hidden passion.

The extreme of his detachment is given in the vengeance he takes for his own murder, for now he exists *only* as a stone mask with a dinted nose:

> A rumour just lived in the village—had a faint and bare existence there, as its people had—that when the knife struck home, the faces changed, from faces of pride to faces of anger and pain; also, that when that dangling figure [of Gaspard] was hauled up forty feet above the fountain, they changed again, and bore a cruel look of being avenged, which they would henceforth bear for ever. In the stone face over the great window of the bed chamber where the murder was done, two fine dints were pointed out in the sculptured nose, which everybody recognised, and which nobody had seen of old. [2, xvi]

In Chapter xxiii of the second book, the Marquis' anger reaches its climax when the revolutionaries have seized power and are destroying his château. Appropriately enough, the Marquis is himself consumed in his own rage, symbolized in the scene by the holocaust:

> The château was left to itself to flame and burn. In the roaring and raging of the conflagration, a red-hot wind, driving straight from the infernal regions, seemed to be blowing the edifice away. With the rising and falling of the blaze, the stone faces showed as if they were in torment. When great masses of stone and timber fell, the face with the two dints in the nose became obscured: anon struggled out of the smoke again, as if it were the face of the cruel Marquis, burning at the stake and contending with the fire.

Dickens says "as if it were the face of the cruel Marquis," but indeed the Marquis' face has become stone, and we finally see him in his true aspect, concealed so long behind the mask: "burning at the stake and contending with the fire."

The same synecdochic use of an image to express character or even theme occurs again and again in the *Tale* and in Dickens' other novels. . . . A Dickens novel is like a crossword puzzle, worked out temporally, one item at a time, but existing finally in space, all at once, in a network of interconnections. Joseph Frank has pointed out similar systems in other writers, where "relationships are juxtaposed independently of narrative progress; the full significance of the scene [in Dickens' case, one could say of the whole novel] is given only by the reflexive relations among the units of meaning." In such a novel, foreshadowing is only one part of the reflexive structure. Elements refer both forward and backward, and clusters of associations not only provide a context for new materials, but are themselves influenced by their repetition in varying circumstances, so that foreshadowing is modified in the memory by what it foreshadows. Consider, for example, the gradual accumulation of meaning in the successive reappearances of the Wine-and-Scarecrow motif introduced in the Wine-Shop chapter:

> Those who had been greedy with the staves of the cask, had acquired a tigerish smear about the mouth; and one tall joker so besmirched, his head more out of a long squalid bag of a nightcap than in it, scrawled upon a wall with his finger dipped in muddy wine-lees—BLOOD.

> A narrow winding street, full of offence and stench, with other narrow winding streets diverging, all peopled by rags and nightcaps, and all smelling of rags and nightcaps, and all visible things with a brooding look upon them that looked ill . . . every wind that blew over France shook the rags of the scarecrows in vain, for the birds, fine of song and feather, took no warning. [1. v]

> The rooms [of Monseigneur], though a beautiful scene to look at, and adorned with every device of decoration that the taste and skill of the time could achieve, were, in truth, not a sound business; considered with any reference to the scarecrows in the rags and nightcaps elsewhere (and not so far off, either, but that the watching towers of Notre Dame, almost equidistant from the two extremes, could see them both), they would have been an exceedingly uncomfortable business. . . . [2, vii]

> Saint Antoine had been, that morning, a vast dusky mass of scarecrows heaving to and fro, with frequent gleams of light above the billowy heads, where steel blades and bayonets shone in the sun. [2, xxi]

> Lovely girls; bright women, brown-haired, black-haired, and grey; youths; stalwart men and old; gentle born and peasant born; all red wine for La Guillotine, all daily brought into light from the dark cellars of loathsome prisons, and carried to her through the street to slake her devouring thirst. [3, v]

Rags, nightcaps, patched scarecrows, greedy drinkers of wine—all change, from signs of poverty, to causes of revolution, to effects of revolution. In this change a kind of temporal succession is implied; however, the meaning of these relations among the images finally exists not in a sequence but rather all at once, "spatially" configured. . . .

 . . . [I]n *A Tale of Two Cities,* Chapter VI of the second book contains . . . a synecdochic foreshadowing, from which the lines of correspondence stretch out both forward and backward to encompass the whole novel. The passage, long as it is, must be quoted nearly in full to preserve its peculiar effect:

> The night was so very sultry, that although they sat with doors and windows open, they were overpowered by heat. When the tea-table was done with, they all moved to one of the windows, and looked out into the heavy twilight. Lucie sat by her father; Darnay sat beside her; Carton leaned against a window. The curtains were long and white, and some of the thunder-gusts that whirled into the corner, caught them up to the ceiling, and waved them like spectral wings.
>
> "The rain-drops are still falling, large, heavy, and few," said Doctor Manette. "It comes slowly."
>
> "It comes surely," said Carton.
>
> They spoke low, as people watching and waiting mostly do; as people in a dark room, watching and waiting for Lightning, always do.
>
> There was a great hurry in the streets, of people speeding away to get to shelter before the storm broke; the wonderful corner for echoes resounded with the echoes of footsteps coming and going, yet not a footstep was there.
>
> "A multitude of people, and yet a solitude!" said Darnay, when they had listened for a while.
>
> "Is it not impressive, Mr. Darnay?" asked Lucie. "Sometimes, I have sat here of an evening, until I have fancied—but even the shade of a foolish fancy makes me shudder tonight, when all is so black and solemn—"
>
> "Let us shudder too. We may know what it is."
>
> "It will seem nothing to you. Such whims are only impressive as we originate them, I think; they are not to be communicated. I have sometimes sat alone here of an evening, listening, until I have made the echoes out to be the echoes of all the footsteps that are coming by-and-by into our lives."
>
> "There is a great crowd coming one day into our lives, if that be so," Sydney Carton struck in, in his moody way.
>
> The footsteps were incessant, and the hurry of them became more and more rapid. The corner echoed and re-echoed with the tread of feet; some, as it seemed, under the windows; some, as it seemed, in the room; some coming, some going, some breaking off, some stopping altogether; all in the distant streets, and not one within sight.

"Are all these footsteps destined to come to all of us, Miss Manette, or are we to divide them among us?"

"I don't know, Mr. Darnay; I told you it was a foolish fancy, but you asked for it. When I have yielded myself to it, I have been alone, and then I have imagined them the footsteps of the people who are to come into my life, and my father's."

"I take them into mine!" said Carton. "*I* ask no questions and make no stipulations. There is a great crowd bearing down upon us, Miss Manette, and I see them—by the Lightning." He added the last words, after there had been a vivid flash which had shown him lounging in the window.

"And I hear them!" he added again, after a peal of thunder. "Here they come, fast, fierce, and furious!"

It was the rush and roar of rain that he typified, and it stopped him, for no voice could be heard in it. A memorable storm of thunder and lightning broke with that sweep of water, and there was not a moment's interval in crash, and fire, and rain, until after the moon rose at midnight.

In the first paragraph the still developing relations among the characters are sketched: Doctor Manette, his loyal daughter, her future husband, and, removed from them all, Carton, in a characteristic posture. The mention of "spectral wings" suggests that what follows may not be merely what it seems. And indeed almost every detail— even bits of the syntax—reaches outside the scene. The triad "large, heavy, and few," which Doctor Manette uses to describe the rain, gives place by the end of the scene to "fast, fierce, and furious," and this in turn looks forward to the phrase "headlong, mad, and dangerous," which later in the novel will be used to describe the outbreak of the revolutionary storm. In accord with the quickening tempo implied in this sequence, the tempest begins slowly, if surely, as Doctor Manette and Carton observe. Their remarks parallel those of Defarge and his wife, as they too await the "tempest" and its lightning, in Chapter XVI of the second book:

"It is a long time," repeated his wife; "and when is it not a long time? Vengeance and retribution require a long time; it is the rule."

"It does not take a long time to strike a man with Lightning," said Defarge.

"How long," demanded madame, composedly, "does it take to make and store the lightning? Tell me."

But Defarge has not long to wait, nor does the little group in Soho. The footsteps that echo in the dark room are in a hurry, pounding into their lives. They are the footsteps of the wine-stained feet in St. Antoine, of the blood-stained feet yet to come. Ironically it is Darnay (through whom the others are all involved in the Revolution) who asks whether the footsteps are coming to them as a group or individually. In the end, of course, they are coming not for Lucie or Darnay, but for Carton, and his voluntary acceptance of whatever they may bring exactly forecasts his final acceptance of another's fate. Finally the tempest is upon them. The description looks forward, with its "rush and roar," its "thunder and lightning," to the Revolution scene:

> Saint Antoine had been, that morning, a vast dusky mass of scarecrows heaving to and fro, with frequent gleams of light above the billowy heads, where steel blades and bayonets shone in the sun. A tremendous roar arose from the throat of Saint Antoine, and a forest of naked arms struggled in the air like shrivelled branches of trees in a winter wind: all the fingers convulsively clutching at every weapon or semblance of a weapon that was thrown up from the depths below, no matter how far off.
>
> Who gave them out, whence they last came, where they began, through what agency they crookedly quivered and jerked, scores at a time, over the heads of the crowd, like a kind of lightning, no eye in the throng could have told. [2, XXI]

The "crash, and fire, and rain" also match the three chapters that describe the Revolution: "Echoing Footsteps," "The Sea Still Rises," and "Fire Rises." But most precise of all is the foreshadowing "sweep of water" which, in its rush, "stopped" Carton. Compare his last moments on the scaffold:

> The murmuring of many voices, the upturning of many faces, the pressing on of many footsteps in the outskirts of the crowd, so that it swells forward in a mass, *like one great heave of water,* all flashes away. [italics mine]

Even Carton's final resurrection is hinted in the rising of the moon which ends the storm. In fact, no major movement of the novel is without its reflection in this scene—the introduction of characters and of the relations between them; the awaiting of the tempest, the listening to approaching footsteps; the breaking of the storm; Carton's sacrifice, his death, his resurrection.

The basis of the elaborate structural synecdoche we have just been examining is to be found in Dickens' use of details, especially details of setting, as means of establishing clusters of meaning and feeling— which, in this novel, finally resolve themselves into two great polar loci, London and Paris, the tales of the little house in Soho and the streets of St. Antoine. *A Tale of Two Cities* displays in its very title this tendency of all Dickens' later work to polarize into two main locales, around one or the other of which all the action centers. This geographical organization is at the heart of each novel's structure, and on it too depends the powerful sense of atmosphere that is one of Dickens' trademarks. Thus is the "unnecessary detail" of the novels crucially significant in their overall effect. Similarly, the principle of combination and connection that holds these details together in their clusters and larger configurations is contiguity. Metonymically and anaphorically controlled patterns dominate the structure, keeping the materials ordered in what, from one point of view, might seem a rather rigid and artificial rhetorical frame. This same principle may be seen operating on every level of the style, articulating sentence and paragraph, episode and plot; characters are built on it, and setting is everywhere determined by it. Artificial as Dickens' rhetoric may sometimes seem, it allows him to command effects which are out of the question for most writers, at once realistic in kind and in quantity of detail, and almost allegorical in the schematization and intensity of rendering. The blend is dreamlike, hallucinatory, super-real. Dickens seems to have tapped a source of imaginative truth which, although it surely corresponds to modes of perception and feeling in all men, has rarely been exploited for literary purposes with any success, and has still more rarely given rise to so full and elaborate a fictive world.

PART TWO

View Points

George Bernard Shaw: From the Preface to Man and Superman

That the author of Everyman was no mere artist, but an artist-philosopher, and that the artist-philosophers are the only sort of artists I take quite seriously, will be no news to you. Even Plato and Boswell, as the dramatists who invented Socrates and Dr Johnson, impress me more deeply than the romantic playwrights. Ever since, as a boy, I first breathed the air of the transcendental regions at a performance of Mozart's Zauberflöte, I have been proof against the garish splendors and alcoholic excitements of the ordinary stage combinations of Tappertitian romance with the police intelligence. Bunyan, Blake, Hogarth, and Turner (these four apart and above all the English classics), Goethe, Shelley, Schopenhauer, Wagner, Ibsen, Morris, Tolstoy, and Nietzsche are among the writers whose peculiar sense of the world I recognize as more as less akin to my own. Mark the word peculiar. I read Dickens and Shakespear without shame or stint; but their pregnant observations and demonstrations of life are not co-ordinated into any philosophy or religion; on the contrary, Dickens's sentimental assumptions are violently contradicted by his observations; and Shakespear's pessimism is only his wounded humanity. Both have the specific genius of the fictionist and the common sympathies of human feeling and thought in pre-eminent degree. They are often saner and shrewder than the philosophers just as Sancho Panza was often saner and shrewder than Don Quixote. They clear away vast masses of oppressive gravity by their sense of the ridiculous, which is at bottom a combination of sound moral judgment with lighthearted good humor. But they are concerned with the diversities of the world instead of with its unities: they are so irreligious that they exploit popular religion for professional purposes without delicacy or scruple (for example, Sydney Carton and the ghost in Hamlet!): they are anarchical, and cannot balance their exposures of Angelo and Dogberry, Sir Leicester Dedlock and Mr. Tite Barnacle, with any portrait of a prophet or a worthy

leader: they have no constructive ideas: they regard those who have
them as dangerous fanatics: in all their fictions there is no leading
thought or inspiration for which any man could conceivably risk the
spoiling of his hat in a shower, much less his life. Both are alike forced
to borrow motives for the more strenuous actions of their personages
from the common stockpot of melodramatic plots; so that Hamlet has
to be stimulated by the prejudices of a policeman and Macbeth by
the cupidities of a bushranger. Dickens, without the excuse of having
to manufacture motives for Hamlets and Macbeths, superflously punts
his crew down the stream of his monthly parts by mechanical devices
which I leave you to describe, my own memory being quite baffled
by the simplest question as to Monks in Oliver Twist, or the long lost
parentage of Smike, or the relations between the Dorrit and Clennam
families so inopportunely discovered by Monsieur Rigaud Blandois.
The truth is, the world was to Shakespear a great "stage of fools" on
which he was utterly bewildered. He could see no sort of sense in living
at all; and Dickens saved himself from the despair of the dream in The
Chimes by taking the world for granted and busying himself with its
details. Neither of them could do anything with a serious positive
character: they could place a human figure before you with perfect
verisimilitude; but when the moment came for making it live and
move, they found, unless it made them laugh, that they had a puppet
on their hands, and had to invent some artificial external stimulus to
make it work.

George Orwell: From "Charles Dickens"

Dickens deals with revolution in the narrower sense in two novels,
Barnaby Rudge and *A Tale of Two Cities.* In *Barnaby Rudge* it is a
case of rioting rather than revolution. The Gordon Riots of 1780,
though they had religious bigotry as a pretext, seem to have been little
more than a pointless outburst of looting. Dickens's attitude to this
kind of thing is sufficiently indicated by the fact that his first idea was
to make the ringleaders of the riots three lunatics escaped from an
asylum. He was dissuaded from this, but the principal figure of the
book is in fact a village idiot. In the chapters dealing with the riots
Dickens shows a most profound horror of mob violence. He delights in
describing scenes in which the "dregs" of the population behave with
atrocious bestiality. These chapters are of great psychological interest,
because they show how deeply he had brooded on this subject. The

From "Charles Dickens," in Dickens, Dali, and Others *by George Orwell (New
York: Reynal and Hitchcock, 1946), pp. 10–16. Copyright © 1946 by George Orwell.
Reprinted by permission of Harcourt Brace Jovanovich, Inc.*

things he describes can only have come out of his imagination, for no riots on anything like the same scale had happened in his lifetime. Here is one of his descriptions, for instance:

> If Bedlam gates had been flung open wide, there would not have issued forth such maniacs as the frenzy of that night had made. There were men there who danced and trampled on the beds of flowers as though they trod down human enemies, and wrenched them from their stalks, like savages who twisted human necks. There were men who cast their lighted torches in the air, and suffered them to fall upon their heads and faces, blistering the skin with deep unseemly burns. There were men who rushed up to the fire, and paddled in it with their hands as if in water; and others who were restrained by force from plunging in, to gratify their deadly longing. On the skull of one drunken lad—not twenty, by his looks—who lay upon the ground with a bottle to his mouth, the lead from the roof came streaming down in a shower of liquid fire, white hot, melting his head like wax. . . . But of all the howling throng not one learnt mercy from, or sickened at, these sights; nor was the fierce, besotted, senseless rage of one man glutted.

You might almost think you were reading a description of "Red" Spain by a partisan of General Franco. One ought, of course, to remember that when Dickens was writing, the London "mob" still existed. (Nowadays there is no mob, only a flock.) Low wages and the growth and shift of population had brought into existence a huge, dangerous slum-proletariat, and until the early middle of the nineteenth century there was hardly such a thing as a police force. When the brickbats began to fly there was nothing between shuttering your windows and ordering the troops to open fire. In *A Tale of Two Cities* he is dealing with a revolution which was really *about* something, and Dickens's attitude is different, but not entirely different. As a matter of fact, *A Tale of Two Cities* is a book which tends to leave a false impression behind, especially after a lapse of time.

The one thing that everyone who has read *A Tale of Two Cities* remembers is the Reign of Terror. The whole book is dominated by the guillotine—tumbrils thundering to and fro, bloody knives, heads bouncing into the basket, and sinister old women knitting as they watch. Actually these scenes only occupy a few chapters, but they are written with terrible intensity, and the rest of the book is rather slow going. But *A Tale of Two Cities* is not a companion volume to *The Scarlet Pimpernel*. Dickens sees clearly enough that the French Revolution was bound to happen and that many of the people who were executed deserved what they got. If, he says, you behave as the French aristocracy had behaved, vengeance will follow. He repeats this over and over again. We are constantly being reminded that while "my lord" is lolling in bed, with four liveried footmen serving his chocolate and the peasants starving outside, somewhere in the forest a tree is grow-ing which will presently be sawn into planks for the platform of the guillotine, etc. etc. etc. The inevitability of the Terror, given its causes, is insisted upon in the clearest terms:

> It was too much the way . . . to talk of this terrible Revolution as if it were the only harvest ever known under the skies that had not been sown—as if nothing had ever been done, or omitted to be done, that had led to it—as if observers of the wretched millions in France, and of the misused and perverted resources that should have made them prosper-ous, had not seen it inevitably coming, years before, and had not in plain terms recorded what they saw.

And again:

> All the devouring and insatiate monsters imagined since imagination could record itself, are fused in the one realisation, Guillotine. And yet there is not in France, with its rich variety of soil and climate, a blade, a leaf, a root, a sprig, a peppercorn, which will grow to maturity under conditions more certain than those that have produced this horror. Crush humanity out of shape once more, under similar hammers, and it will twist itself into the same tortured forms.

In other words, the French aristocracy had dug their own graves. But there is no perception here of what is now called historic necessity. Dickens sees that the results are inevitable, given the causes, but he thinks that the causes might have been avoided. The Revolution is something that happens because centuries of oppression have made the French peasantry sub-human. If the wicked nobleman could some-how have turned over a new leaf, like Scrooge, there would have been no Revolution, no *jacquerie*, no guillotine—and so much the better. This is the opposite of the "revolutionary" attitude. From the "revolu-tionary" point of view the class-struggle is the main source of progress, and therefore the nobleman who robs the peasant and goads him to revolt is playing a necessary part, just as much as the Jacobin who guillotines the nobleman. Dickens never writes anywhere a line that can be interpreted as meaning this. Revolution as he sees it is merely a monster that is begotten by tyranny and always ends by devouring its own instruments. In Sidney Carton's vision at the foot of the guil-lotine, he foresees Defarge and the other leading spirits of the Terror all perishing under the same knife—which, in fact, was approximately what happened.

And Dickens is very sure that revolution *is* a monster. That is why everyone remembers the revolutionary scenes in *A Tale of Two Cities;* they have the quality of nightmare, and it is Dickens's own nightmare. Again and again he insists upon the meaningless horrors of revolution —the mass-butcheries, the injustice, the ever-present terror of spies, the frightful bloodlust of the mob. The descriptions of the Paris mob —the description, for instance, of the crowd of murderers struggling round the grindstone to sharpen their weapons before butchering the prisoners in the September massacres—outdo anything in *Barnaby Rudge*. The revolutionaries appear to him simply as degraded savages —in fact, as lunatics. He broods over their frenzies with a curious imaginative intensity. He describes them dancing the "Carmagnole," for instance:

> There could not be fewer than five hundred people, and they were dancing like five thousand demons. . . . They danced to the popular Revolution song, keeping a ferocious time that was like a gnashing of teeth in unison. . . . They advanced, retreated, struck at one another's hands, clutched at one another's heads, spun round alone, caught one another, and spun round in pairs, until many of them dropped. . . . Suddenly they stopped again, paused, struck out the time afresh, forming into lines the width of the public way, and, with their heads low down and their hands high up, swooped screaming off. No fight could have been half so terrible as this dance. It was so emphatically a fallen sport—a something, once innocent, delivered over to all devilry.

He even credits some of these wretches with a taste for guillotining children. The passage I have abridged above ought to be read in full. It and others like it show how deep was Dickens's horror of revolutionary hysteria. Notice, for instance, that touch, "with their heads low down and their hands high up," etc., and the evil vision it conveys. Madame Defarge is a truly dreadful figure, certainly Dickens's most successful attempt at a *malignant* character. Defarge and others are simply "the new oppressors who have risen on the destruction of the old," the revolutionary courts are presided over by "the lowest, cruellest and worst populace," and so on and so forth. All the way through Dickens insists upon the nightmare insecurity of a revolutionary period, and in this he shows a great deal of prescience. "A law of the suspected, which struck away all security for liberty or life, and delivered over any good and innocent person to any bad and guilty one; prisons gorged with people who had committed no offence, and could obtain no hearing"—it would apply pretty accurately to several countries to-day.

The apologists of any revolution generally try to minimise its horrors; Dickens's impulse is to exaggerate them—and from a historical point of view he has certainly exaggerated. Even the Reign of Terror was a much smaller thing than he makes it appear. Though he quotes no figures, he gives the impression of a frenzied massacre lasting for years, whereas in reality the whole of the Terror, so far as the number of deaths goes, was a joke compared with one of Napoleon's battles. But the bloody knives and the tumbrils rolling to and fro create in his mind a special, sinister vision which he has succeeded in passing on to generations of readers. Thanks to Dickens, the very word "tumbril" has a murderous sound; one forgets that a tumbril is only a sort of farm-cart. To this day, to the average Englishman, the French Revolution means no more than a pyramid of severed heads. It is a strange thing that Dickens, much more in sympathy with the ideas of the Revolution than most Englishmen of his time, should have played a part in creating this impression.

Sergei Eisenstein: From *Dickens, Griffith, and the Film Today*

The visual images of Dickens are inseparable from aural images. The English philosopher and critic, George Henry Lewes, though puzzled as to its significance, recorded that "Dickens once declared to me that every word said by his characters was distinctly *heard* by him. . . ."

We can see for ourselves that his descriptions offer not only absolute *accuracy of detail,* but also an absolutely *accurate drawing of the behavior* and actions of his characters. And this is just as true for the most trifling details of behavior—even gesture, as it is for the basic generalized characteristics of the image. Isn't this piece of description of Mr. Dombey's behavior actually an exhaustive regisseur-actor directive?

> He had already laid his hand upon the bell-rope to convey his usual summons to Richards, when his eye fell upon a writing-desk, belonging to his deceased wife, which had been taken, among other things, from a cabinet in her chamber. It was not the first time that his eye had lighted on it. He carried the key in his pocket; and he brought it to his table and opened it now—having previously locked the room door— with a well-accustomed hand.

Here the last phrase arrests one's attention: there is a certain awkwardness in its description. However, this "inserted" phrase: *having previously locked the room door,* "fitted in" as if recollected by the author in the middle of a later phrase, instead of being placed where it apparently should have been, in the consecutive order of the description, that is, before the words, *and he brought it to his table,* is found exactly at this spot for quite *un*fortuitous reasons.

From "Dickens, Griffith, and the Film Today," in Film Form by Sergei Eisenstein, edited and translated by Jay Leyda (New York: Harcourt, Brace and Company, Inc., 1949), pp. 211–16. Copyright © by Harcourt Brace Jovanovich, Inc. and reprinted with their permission.

In this deliberate "montage" displacement of the time-continuity of the description there is a brilliantly caught rendering of the *transient thievery* of the action, slipped between the preliminary action and the act of reading another's letter, carried out with that absolute "correctness" of gentlemanly dignity which Mr. Dombey knows how to give to any behavior or action of his.

This very (montage) arrangement of the phrasing gives an exact direction to the "performer," so that in defining this decorous and confident opening of the writing-desk, he must "play" the closing and locking of the door with a hint of an entirely different shade of conduct. And it would be this "shading" in which would also be played the unfolding of the letter; but in this part of the "performance" Dickens makes this shading more precise, not only with a significant arrangement of the words, but also with an exact description of characteristics.

> From beneath a heap of torn and cancelled scraps of paper, he took one letter that remained entire. Involuntarily holding his breath as he opened this document, and 'bating in the stealthy action something of his arrogant demeanour, he sat down, resting his head upon one hand, and read it through.

The reading itself is done with a shading of absolutely gentlemanly cold decorum:

> He read it slowly and attentively, and with a nice particularity to every syllable. Otherwise than as his great deliberation seemed unnatural, and perhaps the result of an effort equally great, he allowed no sign of emotion to escape him. When he had read it through, he folded and refolded it slowly several times, and tore it carefully into fragments. Checking his hand in the act of throwing these away, he put them in his pocket, as if unwilling to trust them even to the chances of being reunited and deciphered; and instead of ringing, as usual, for little Paul, he sat solitary all the evening in his cheerless room.

This scene does not appear in the final version of the novel, for with the aim of increasing the tension of the action, Dickens cut out this passage on Forster's advice; in his biography of Dickens Forster preserved this passage to show with what mercilessness Dickens sometimes "cut" writing that had cost him great labor. This mercilessness once more emphasizes that sharp clarity of representation towards which Dickens strove by all means, endeavoring with purely cinematic laconism to say what he considered necessary. (This, by the way, did not in the least prevent his novels from achieving enormous breadth.)

I don't believe I am wrong in lingering on this example, for one need only alter two or three of the character names and change

Dickens's name to the name of the hero of my essay, in order to impute literally almost everything told here to the account of Griffith.

From that steely, observing glance, which I remember from my meeting with him, to the capture *en passant* of key details or tokens—indications of character, Griffith has all this in as much a Dickens-esque sharpness and clarity as Dickens, on his part, had cinematic "optical quality," "frame composition," "close-up," and the alteration of emphasis by special lenses.

Analogies and resemblances cannot be pursued too far—they lose conviction and charm. They begin to take on the air of machination or card-tricks. I should be very sorry to lose the conviction of the affinity between Dickens and Griffith, allowing this abundance of common traits to slide into a game of anecdotal semblance of tokens.

All the more that such a gleaning from Dickens goes beyond the limits of interest in Griffith's individual cinematic craftsmanship and widens into a concern with film-craftmanship in general. This is why I dig more and more deeply into the film-indications of Dickens, revealing them through Griffith—for the use of future film-exponents. So I must be excused, in leafing through Dickens, for having found in him even—a "dissolve." How else could this passage be defined—the opening of the last chapter of *A Tale of Two Cities:*

> Along the Paris streets, the death-carts rumble, hollow and harsh. Six tumbrils carry the day's wine to La Guillotine. . . .
> Six tumbrils roll along the streets. Change these back again to what they were, thou powerful enchanter, Time, and they shall be seen to be the carriages of absolute monarchs, the equipages of feudal nobles, the toilettes of flaring Jezebels, the churches that are not my Father's house but dens of thieves, the huts of millions of starving peasants!

How many such "cinematic" surprises must be hiding in Dickens's pages!

However, let us turn to the basic montage structure, whose rudiment in Dickens's work was developed into the elements of film composition in Griffith's work. Lifting a corner of the veil over these riches, these hitherto unused experiences, let us look into *Oliver Twist.* Open it at the twenty-first chapter. Let's read its beginning:

Chapter XXI [1]

1. It was a cheerless morning when they got into the street; blowing and raining hard; and the clouds looking dull and stormy.

The night had been very wet: for large pools of water had collected in the road: and the kennels were overflowing.

---

[1] For demonstration purposes I have broken this beginning of the chapter into smaller pieces than did its author; the numbering is, of course, also mine.

There was a faint glimmering of the coming day in the sky; but it rather aggravated than relieved the gloom of the scene: the sombre light only serving to pale that which the street lamps afforded, without shedding any warmer or brighter tints upon the wet housetops, and dreary streets.

There appeared to be nobody stirring in that quarter of the town; for the windows of the houses were all closely shut; and the streets through which they passed, were noiseless and empty.

2. By the time they had turned into the Bethnal Green Road, the day had fairly begun to break. Many of the lamps were already extinguished;
a few country waggons were slowly toiling on, towards London;
and now and then, a stage-coach, covered with mud, rattled briskly by:
the driver bestowing, as he passed, an admonitory lash upon the heavy waggoner who, by keeping on the wrong side of the road, had endangered his arriving at the office, a quarter of a minute after his time.

The public-houses, with gas-lights burning inside, were already open.

By degrees, other shops began to be unclosed; and a few scattered people were met with.

Then, came straggling groups of labourers going to their work;
then, men and women with fish-baskets on their heads:
donkey-carts laden with vegetables;
chaise-carts filled with live-stock or whole carcasses of meat;
milk-women with pails;
and an unbroken concourse of people, trudging out with various supplies to the eastern suburbs of the town.

3. As they approached the City, the noise and traffic gradually increased;
and when they threaded the streets between Shoreditch and Smithfield, it had swelled into a roar of sound and bustle.

It was as light as it was likely to be, till night came on again; and the busy morning of half the London population had begun. . . .

4. It was market-morning.
The ground was covered, nearly ankle-deep, with filth and mire;
and a thick stream, perpetually rising from the reeking bodies of the cattle,
and mingling with the fog,
which seemed to rest upon the chimney-tops, hung heavily above. . . .
Countrymen,
butchers,
drovers,
hawkers,
boys,
thieves,
idlers,
and vagabonds of every low grade,
were mingled together in a dense mass;

5. the whistling of drovers,
the barking of dogs,
the bellowing and plunging of oxen,
the bleating of sheep,
the grunting and squeaking of pigs;
the cries of hawkers,
the shouts, oaths and quarrelling on all sides;
the ringing of bells
and roar of voices, that issued from every public-house;
the crowding, pushing, driving, beating,
whooping and yelling;
the hideous and discordant din that resounded from every corner of
the market;
and the unwashed, unshaken, squalid, and dirty figures constantly
running to and fro, and bursting in and out of the throng; rendered it a
stunning and bewildering scene, which quite confounded the senses.

How often have we encountered just such a structure in the work
of Griffith? This austere accumulation and quickening tempo, this
gradual play of light: from burning street-lamps, to their being extinguished; from night, to dawn; from dawn, to the full radiance of
day (*It was as light as it was likely to be, till night came on again*);
this calculated transition from purely visual elements to an inter-
weaving of them with aural elements: at first as an indefinite rumble,
coming from afar at the second stage of increasing light, so that the
rumble may grow into a roar, transferring us to a purely aural structure, now concrete and objective (section 5 of our break-down); with
such scenes, picked up *en passant,* and intercut into the whole—like
the driver, hastening towards his office; and finally, these magnifi-
cently typical details, the reeking bodies of the cattle, from which the
steam rises and mingles with the over-all cloud of morning fog, or
the close-up of the legs in the almost ankle-deep filth and mire, all
this gives the fullest cinematic sensation of the panorama of a market.

A. O. J. Cockshut: From *The Imagination of Charles Dickens*

In *Barnaby Rudge* and in *A Tale of Two Cities* Dickens caused
two of the dominating images of his literary life to clash. The crowd
makes war on the prison. In these passages we are aware of a very
deep excitement in the author, as if this was his own private version
of the meeting of irresistible force and immovable object. If examined

From The Imagination of Charles Dickens, *by A. O. J. Cockshut (New York:
New York University Press, 1962), pp. 32–36, 81–83, 185–86. Copyright © 1961 by
A. O. J. Cockshut. Reprinted by permission of New York University Press.*

in association with *Oliver Twist,* the prison chapters [in *A Tale of Two Cities*] read almost like a reply to the superficiality of Fagin's death scene. If prison is only the temporary detention of the innocent boy, who is sure to be saved in the end, or the horrible but just punishment of the thoroughly evil man, much of its terror disappears. But in *A Tale of Two Cities* it is a great deal more than this. Manette has been released from "105 North Tower," the royalist prison, and is living in the house of the revolutionary plotter, Defarge. He is free, but his freedom means nothing to him. He is always alone, and can scarcely bear visitors. He requires to be locked in his room, "because he has lived so long locked up, that he would be frightened—rave, tear himself to pieces—die—come to I know not what harm, if his door was left open."

He has forgotten his name, but remembers perpetually the number of his prison room, and he still occupies himself with the manual work he did in prison. But worse, he has not only forgotten himself as a human being, he has been virtually forgotten by his benefactors. Defarge does not pity him as a kind of dead trophy or example to stir up revolutionary feeling. So influential is Defarge's view of him that it momentarily infects even Manette's daughter.

"I am afraid of it."
"Of it? Of what?"
"I mean of him . . . of my father."

We miss the point if we read this merely as a description of callous perversity. On the contrary, when the prisoner is described by the author, he appears in much the same light. "He, and his old canvas frock, and his loose stockings, and all his poor tatters of clothes, had, in a long seclusion from direct light and air, faded down to such a dull uniformity of parchment-yellow, that it would have been hard to say which was which." Here is Dickens's ultimate in misery, a suffering that cannot be relieved, pitied or understood, that is not aware of itself, and to the question "I hope you care to be recalled to life?" can only answer "I can't say."

And to make us universalise the picture, and apply it to the suffering world in general, Dickens placed at the end of the chapter this image: "Beneath that arch of unmoved and eternal lights; some, so remote from this little earth that the learned tell us it is doubtful whether their rays have even yet discovered it, as a point in space where anything is suffered or done. . . ."

In this chapter, Dickens achieved something new. He used the image of the prison for a steady gaze, without self-pity or hysteria, at the general miseries of life. For although Manette can recover his wits and his human dignity, the prison is lurking within him, ready to regain control, when a new emotional crisis occurs. At the time of his daughter's marriage he goes back to his unconscious shoemaking. Perhaps this incident has a somewhat unreal and contrived air. But its importance in the author's development is nevertheless considerable. Dickens was, as we have seen, exceptionally aware of external objects; his imagination was extraordinarily literal; his psychological grasp, which was eventually to become formidable, was slow to develop. His natural tendency, therefore, was to blame all the misery he observed on circumstances, on tyrants, on social conditions. So it was bound to take time for him to comprehend that the prison he was endlessly seeking to describe and understand was, in part, the mental creation of the prisoner, that to strike away the chains and fetters could not solve all the prisoner's problems. Having now realised this, having arrived at his own version of the discovery:

> O the mind, mind has mountains; cliffs of fall
> Frightful, sheer, no-man fathomed.

he was eventually able to develop it in the case of Miss Havisham into a deep psychological study.

But it may be objected that all this special pleading does not improve the quality of the actual scene in which Manette returns to his shoemaking, if, as I have suggested, that is deficient. And, of course, that is true. Dickens was, in his way, a great artist, but he was never a pure artist. Aspects of his mind, interesting in themselves, but structurally irrelevant, are always liable to break in. But sometimes, as here, we can have the satisfaction of feeling that the imperfections contribute to the making of later and better works.

The consequences of Manette's hopeless misery are very instructive. When the Revolution comes, his long years of imprisonment under the old régime entitle Manette to a privileged position. He can use his influence on behalf of his accused son-in-law; and he can even say "It all tended to a good end, my friend; it was not mere waste and ruin." When these hopes seem to be fulfilled, he is a proud and happy man. But the release of Evrémonde is only temporary. He is once again denounced and sentenced to death. The melodramatic ending in which Evrémonde is saved by the substitution of Carton, cannot obscure the significance of this. For Evrémonde's second condemnation is occasioned by the reading of a document written by Manette in prison. The supposed utility of those long years in prison ends in disillusionment. And at this point, with sombre appropriateness, Manette returns, as Dorrit had done so much more convincingly, to the imbecile mode of consciousness which possessed him in his prison years.

So the direct and tangible value of prisoners' suffering is implicitly denied. But there is still a strange dignity in the prison, which comes to Evrémonde as a surprise:

"In the instinctive association of prisoners with shameful crimes and disgrace, the newcomer recoiled from his company. But the crowning unreality of his long unreal ride, was, their all at once rising to receive him, with every refinement of manner known to the time, and with all the engaging graces and courtesies of life."

No doubt Dickens had read of some such scene in the French Revolution, but all the same, this dignity had personal significance also for him. It reduces the prison to a terror of manageable proportions. If it cannot be called a complete moral or artistic answer to the problem of the prison which he carried with him through his writing life, it at least contains no cheat or deception. He was making progress.

. . . It is not surprising, given Dickens's comparative immaturity at the time, and the degree to which his personal emotions were involved, that the end of *Barnaby Rudge* should be unsatisfactory. His deepest meditations on the prison would come many years later in *Little Dorrit,* while he would develop an interest in a different, more civilised type of crowd. In *Barnaby Rudge* there is a mighty clash, but no tragedy and no reconciliation.

It would be pleasant and convenient in this study where the main stress falls on Dickens's development, to point to a later work where this clash of great ideas led up to a satisfying climax and resolution. But no writer's career, certainly not the career of Dickens, is as neat and regular as critics are inclined to wish. In some ways, the crowd of *Barnaby Rudge* remains the most memorable that Dickens ever described. Yet there were developments, even if they were not all necessarily improvements. In *A Tale of Two Cities,* he contrived to give a keener impression of an invisible crowd, of mounting communal passions nursed in secret which must one day overthrow the government. Dickens had little of importance to say about the meaning of political revolution. But he was able, especially by the use of images of darkness, to convey a fine glimpse of slowly nurtured social forces coming to catastrophic fruition.

> Darkness closed around, and then came the ringing of the church bells and the distant beating of the military drums in the Palace Court-Yard, as the women sat knitting, knitting. Darkness encompassed them. Another darkness was closing in as surely, when the church bells, then ringing pleasantly in many an airy steeple over France, should be melted into thundering cannon. . . . So much was closing in about the women who sat knitting, knitting, that they their very selves were closing in around a structure yet unbuilt, where they were to sit knitting, knitting, counting dropping heads.

Dickens never repeated these vast spectacular crowd scenes. His mind turned to different versions of the crowd. In *Little Dorrit* and *Our Mutual Friend,* the crowds are only a background, the cheerful sufferers of Bleeding Heart Yard, the swarming inhabitants of those sad streets where Arthur Clennam walks on Sundays, and remembers the miseries of his youth.

The crowd and the solitary—there is nothing really surprising in the fact that the same man should concentrate on both. The friendless solitary feels as if the whole of society were an implacable crowd. And the dual preoccupation reminds us of what was missing in Dickens. He did not understand, or at any rate, did not effectively portray family relationships. Like every novelist, of course, he described many families; but did he ever give us a convincing portrait of a marriage? On the subject of the parent-child relationship he is more lucid, but still apt to be perverse. He tends to reverse the roles. Little Dorrit is a mother to her father, not a daughter. The doll's dressmaker in *Our Mutual Friend* is a stern and terrifying stepmother to her father. Even friendship tends to develop into an unreal jollity.

Now, of course, Dickens is, or was once, a great author for family reading. And he was revered in his time, and has sometimes been attacked since, as a fanatical celebrator of the family affections. But this is deceptive. The Dickens family is not the fundamental Christian and Freudian family of father, mother and children. It is a covey of aunts, and cousins and relatives by marriage. His favorite family celebration is Christmas. That is, in England, just when the basic Christian and Freudian family is least itself, when it is a confused jumble of three or four generations, in fact, when it becomes a *crowd.*

So it is that the idea of the crowd (and the corresponding idea of the solitary) are fundamental for Dickens. They are the key to his unrivalled strength as a portrayer of industrial society, the home of crowds. They are the source of his weakness in presenting deep personal relationships. And since the deepest human affections, if denied proper expression, will become muddled and distorted, his sentimentality also can be referred to the same source. . . .

Nearly all the most popular literary works of the nineteenth century were melodramas. *Murder in the Red Barn, Lady Audley's Secret,* Carlyle's *French Revolution* and Macaulay's history differ widely in quality, no doubt, but they were all very popular, and all intensely melodramatic. Now, as we have seen, one of Dickens's leading ideas, involved with some of his best, and some of his worst devices of plot, was that we are members one of another. Solemnly consecrated though this idea is by religious tradition, in literary terms it is very closely related to melodrama. Coincidences, long-lost sons, buried wills, hidden relationships—all these are crude statements of the idea that we are linked much more closely than we realise with people we have never seen. Vulgar in his tastes, and towering in imagination, Dickens seized eagerly upon the ridiculous paraphernalia of English melodrama. He enjoyed over-obvious comparisons, like the wine running through the gutters and foreshadowing the blood bath of the Revolution in *A Tale of Two Cities.*

But the melodrama Dickens at first so carelessly copied was capable of enormous development, for its simple stock of ideas has very deep psychological roots. What could be more naïve and melodramatic, and at the same time more subtle and serious than the following passage from *Great Expectations?* The child Pip is watching the terrifying convict depart:

> As I saw him go, picking his way among the nettles, and among the brambles that bound the green mounds, he looked in my young eyes as if he were eluding the hands of dead people, stretching up cautiously out of their graves, to get a twist upon his ankle and pull him in.

We have all read articles about the influence of heredity on crime. But this idea, which we associate, perhaps rather wearily with "social science," here plunges down to a far deeper mental level, the level at which artistic appeals are made. And the means by which it reaches this point of depth is very near to the traditional macabre and childish melodrama. Dickens was at the same time a rather naïve conservative-liberal reformer, a lover of the fantastic, and an original artist fashioning new symbolic equivalents for our most inarticulate emotions. It is in this cluster of contradictions that much of the fascination of his work resides.

His slowness to grasp general ideas did not prove a handicap to the kind of achievements for which he was best fitted. Symbolic meanings seep slowly through the mass of accumulated detail, the wonderful topographical intimacy, the jostling contemporary problems. Gigantic failures like Melville's "Pierre" bear witness how ill-fitted the novel is to bear a condition where the idea triumphs and the fact is defeated. The ambiguities of Dickens's river in *Our Mutual Friend* or the slowly-developing meaning of the sea in *Dombey and Son* are only tolerable because they merge hesitantly out of an undeniable physical reality.

So, in the end, his lack of intellectual consistency, already castigated in these pages, and the neurotic instability of the man's feelings, hardly matter, because the vivid journalist, the entertainer and the artist are triumphantly at one.

Taylor Stoehr: From *Dickens: The Dreamer's Stance*

In a "realistic" novel—say Jane Austen's *Emma*—the selection and ordering of details is what we might call "socially" or "conventionally" determined; many details seem to have been omitted, as irrelevant or uninteresting ("unnecessary" in Orwell's terms); and those actually selected seem to be arranged and presented with a view to expressing a particular attitude, a notion of what is important—all of which gives rise to the reader's feeling that things "add up," that one thing leads to another in an organic way. Thus, appropriate as it may seem to call her method "realism," Jane Austen's contriving intelligence is in evidence at every point, shaping and arranging things with careful artifice. We feel her presence in the abstraction and orientation. It is, in fact, essential to the realistic effect that we be aware of the narrator in reading *Emma* or *Pride and Prejudice.* With Dickens the situation is quite different. There is little apparent abstraction (and thus little apparent choosing), and the ordering is of a very peculiar sort—artificial in such a way as to strike us as even mechanical. The order given in devices such as anaphora is imposed from above, like the grid used in interpreting an aerial photograph, so that the elements do not seem to add up or move in a particular direction, but rather to exist all at once, articulated without being integrated, ordered without being organized. The detail is not presented according to principles that foster a sense of growth and change in time, the essence of realistic plot and character. Instead, the method involves a halting of time, a freezing of the scene to allow "photographic accuracy" in the representation of life-going-on. This is exactly comparable to the timeless quality of the present-tense narrative in *Bleak House,* with its immediacy and detachment, and its impassive camera-eye narrator.

Of course there is some direction and progress in even the most ornamental of Dickens' scenes. But this orientation rarely arises from the rhetorical ordering; it is usually embedded in the details themselves, which only *seem* to be accidental and unchosen. Thus in the Hunger passage, emotional organization is implied in the way the scene develops, first from Hunger "pushed out of the tall houses, in the wretched clothing," to the Hunger "shred into atomies," then from the "wild-beast thought of the possibility of turning at bay" to the "murderous" gunstocks and "crippling stones of the pavement." This

From "The Vision of Reality," Chapter II of Dickens: The Dreamer's Stance *(Ithaca: Cornell University Press, 1965) pp. 59–65. Copyright © by Cornell University. Used by permission of Cornell University Press. [Numbered footnotes acknowledging Professor Stoehr's scholarly references have been omitted.]*

movement is not inherent in the scene itself (though it appears to be), but is a movement of the narrator's perception, or of his attitude toward what he perceives, as he reads more and more violence into the details before him. The bias of the narrator's intelligence may thus be exposed to our view, but the emotion works only as an undercurrent, subverting the structure of the rhetoric rather than following it. And in any case, the feeling seems to have less to do with the narrator than with the independent existence of the scene itself, with the objects which present themselves because *there they are,* already quivering with life. . . .

When Dickens uses metaphor, we must recognize that he is intruding in the scene. The metaphors of the Hunger passage—the comparison of the street lamps to sea-lamps on a ship, or the comparison of the darkness surrounding the lamps to the darkness of man's condition—clearly show Dickens the narrator stepping in, to comment on the story. Both these metaphors are part of the overt prediction (as distinguished from mere foreshadowing) which Dickens feels so often compelled to introduce in his tales ("For, the time was to come . . ."). It might even be argued that metaphors are invariably to be found in those passages traditionally condemned for their "editorializing" tone, where Dickens sentimentally or angrily or bitterly inserts his own opinion of the world he has created. Such is the basis, for example, of the metaphoric passage in the last chapter of the *Tale:*

> Crush humanity out of shape once more, under similar hammers, and it will twist itself into the same tortured forms. Sow the same seed of rapacious licence and oppression over again, and it will surely yield the same fruit according to its kind.

The oratorical tone that is so unpleasant here marks the author's withdrawal from the story in order to grind his own axe, his rather conventional moral indignation, a declaration of authorial intentions.[1]

And yet, even in metaphor, Dickens' narrative perspective is often maintained in its detachment. The "lamp-light" metaphor in the

---

[1] The problem of irony is not so easily dealt with as that of metaphor. Does the presence of irony necessarily remind us of the narrator? Take the case of *Moll Flanders,* where we are frequently presented with what must be regarded as "unintentional irony." Instances of this sort surely make us aware of the narrator's (Defoe's, not Moll's) presence; but it is not so obvious that *intended* incongruities between states of affairs "expressed" and "implied" will have this effect. The ironic conception of Doctor Manette's part in the denunciation of his son-in-law does not produce any special awareness of the narrator as we read; on the other hand, the harsh, satirical treatment of Stryver may remind us that we are being told a story, by a narrator who has his own thoughts and opinions. Perhaps we could say that Dickens' detachment (and hence the usual narrative perspective) collapses only when the irony veers toward sarcasm, tantamount to a loss of control much as in Defoe's "unintentional irony."

Hunger passage is a good example, for here the setting—basis of most of his metonymies—predominates as usual, so that the comparison seems less invented than stumbled upon. The motion of the lamps seems like the swaying of ship-lanterns at sea, which in turn reminds us of tempest, ship, and crew (connection by contiguity), and from these we are referred back again metaphorically to the state of France, its being at sea and in danger of tempest. Dickens' tendency is to extend his metaphors, chiefly by metonymic attachment of the related circumstances, until the original comparison becomes almost mythic, often with something like a plot line relating the separate elements of the expanded correspondence. Consider, for example, the further development of this "lamp-light" metaphor, which becomes a full-fledged "sea" metaphor in Dickens' description of the Revolution (2, XXI):

> As a whirlpool of boiling waters has a centre point, so, all this raging circled round Defarge's wine-shop, and every human drop in the caldron had a tendency to be sucked towards the vortex. . . .

> With a roar that sounded as if all the breath in France had been shaped into the detested word ["Bastille"], the living sea rose, wave on wave, depth on depth, and overflowed the city to that point. Alarm-bells ringing, drums beating, the sea raging and thundering on its new beach, the attack begun.

> . . . Suddenly the sea rose immeasurably wider and higher, and swept Defarge of the wine-shop over the lowered drawbridge, past the massive stone outer walls, in among the eight great towers surrendered!

> So resistless was the force of the ocean bearing him on, that even to draw his breath or turn his head was as impracticable as if he had been struggling in the surf at the South Sea. . . .

> . . . So tremendous was the noise of the living ocean, in its irruption into the Fortress, and its inundation of the courts and passages and staircases. All around outside, too, it beat the walls with a deep, hoarse roar, from which, occasionally, some partial shouts of tumult broke and leaped into the air like spray.

> The sea of black and threatening waters, and of destructive upheaving of wave against wave, whose depths were yet unfathomed and whose forces were yet unknown. The remorseless sea of turbulently swaying shapes, voices of vengeance, and faces hardened in the furnaces of suffering until the touch of pity could make no mark on them.

The completeness and inner consistency of the metaphor, as it is extended and expanded to constitute a world in itself, seem to lift the figure out of the realm of metaphor altogether. We believe in the metaphor as though it were not a metaphor at all. The power of such

figures to compel belief is beyond rhetoric, as Ernst Cassirer has suggested in *Language and Myth:*

> For mythic thinking there is much more in metaphor than a bare
> "substitution," a mere rhetorical figure of speech; . . . what seems to
> our subsequent reflection as a sheer transcription is mythically conceived
> as a genuine and direct identification.

All of Dickens' major metaphors—the widely discussed symbols which
lie at the center of his didactic concerns in the novels—have this
"mythic" quality. Pestilence and tempest, court and prison, factory
and slum, these are more than mere metaphors for aspects of society;
they *are* aspects of society. The dust-heaps in *Our Mutual Friend* do
not merely represent wealth, nor is their function simply to establish
the psychological relation between money and excrement: rather an
identity is posited—money is excrement, "gold-dust." Similarly
the sea-mob in *A Tale of Two Cities,* the scarecrow-citizens of Saint
Antoine, the blood-wine on the cobblestones—in varying degrees
these figures have transcended metaphor to become dreamlike amal-
gams of object and feeling. The effect is weirdly hallucinatory, rather
more like dream than myth. Objects are exhaustively described with
the vividness of detail characteristic of dream; the "meanings" of the
objects are also dreamlike, so that things count as passions yet remain things too, in a way that is rarely felt in waking life. Taine made
the point brilliantly a century ago:

> An imagination so lucid and energetic cannot but animate inanimate
> objects without an effort. It provokes in the mind in which it works
> extraordinary emotions, and the author pours over the objects which
> he figures to himself, something of the ever-welling passion which over-
> flows in him. Stones for him take a voice, white walls swell out into big
> phantoms, black wells yawn hideously and mysteriously in the darkness;
> legions of strange creatures whirl shuddering over the fantastic land-
> scape; blank nature is peopled, inert matter moves. But the images
> remain clear; in this madness there is nothing vague or disorderly;
> imaginary objects are designed with outlines as precise and details as
> numerous as real objects, and the dream is equal to the reality.

Juggle the last clause and you have it precisely: the reality is that of
dream.

Chronology of Important Dates

	Dickens	The Age
1812	Charles Dickens born February 7, at Portsea near Rochester.	Luddite riots: knitting machines smashed by hand-workers in several shires; death penalties imposed.
1814	Dickens family moves to London.	
1815		Final defeat of Napoleon and restoration of Bourbon dynasty. Corn Law passed to support British wheat prices.
1819		Queen Victoria born. "Peterloo Massacre," armed opposition to assemblage of workers in St. Peter's Fields, Manchester.
1824	John Dickens imprisoned in the Marshalsea for debt; Charles works for a few months in Warren's Blacking Warehouse.	
1824–26	Dickens finishes his schooling at Wellington House Academy.	
1827–28	Works as attorney's clerk, learns shorthand.	
1829–32	Law reporter for Doctor's Commons; general and parliamentary reporter for the *True Sun* and the *Mirror of Parliament*.	
1832		First Reform Bill passed, extending suffrage.

	Dickens	The Age
1833	First publication, a sketch entitled "A Dinner at Poplar Walk," in the *Monthly Magazine*.	Factory Act places restrictions on child labor.
1834	Reporter for the *Morning Chronicle*.	
1836	*Sketches by Boz. Pickwick Papers* begun in monthly parts. Dickens assumes editorship of *Bentley's Miscellany*. Marries Catherine Hogarth.	
1837	*Oliver Twist* begun in monthly parts. First child, Charles, born. Sudden death of Mary Hogarth.	Accession of Queen Victoria. Publication of Carlyle's *French Revolution*.
1838	*Nicholas Nickleby* begun.	Chartism, chiefly a movement to reform parliament and electoral procedures, develops.
1840–41	*The Old Curiosity Shop* and *Barnaby Rudge* published in *Master Humphrey's Clock*.	
1842	Travels and lectures in the United States. *American Notes* published.	Female and child labor in mines prohibited.
1843	*Martin Chuzzlewit* and *A Christmas Carol* published.	Publication of Carlyle's *Past and Present*.
1844–45	Travels in Italy and France. Beginning of amateur theatricals.	
1846	*Dombey and Son* begun.	Corn Laws repealed.
1847		Publication of Thackeray's *Vanity Fair* and J. S. Mill's *Political Economy*.
1848		Revolutions break out all over Europe. Chartist demonstration and petition in London. Collapse of Chartist movement because of divided leadership and gradually improving working conditions.

Dickens	*The Age*
1849–50	*David Copperfield;* Dickens establishes the weekly periodical, *Household Words.*	
1851	Performs with an amateur company before the Queen.	Judicial reforms to improve equity and efficiency of courts begun in a series of parliamentary acts.
1852–53	*Bleak House.*	
1854	Visits Preston to observe effects of a strike in the cotton mills; returns to publish *Hard Times* in *Household Words.*	Crimean War begins; Preston strike ends.
1855	Meeting with Maria Beadnell, his early love (now Maria Winter), excites a flood of anticipation followed by severe emotional disappointment. *Little Dorrit* begun.	
1856	Buys Gad's Hill Place, near Rochester, which will remain his home until death.	Bernard Shaw born.
1857	First public reading from his works. Wilkie Collins's play, *The Frozen Deep,* first performed, with Dickens in the role of the self-sacrificing Richard Wardour. A later performance given for the Queen. Partially recast for still later performance in Manchester; among new participants is Ellen Ternan.	Divorce Act. Publication of *Madame Bovary.*
1858	Announces separation from Catherine, and publishes a statement of explanation on the front page of *Household Words.*	
1859	Brings *Household Words* to a close. Begins new periodical, *All the Year Round,* with *A Tale of Two Cities* in weekly parts (April 20–Nov. 26).	Darwin's *Origin of Species* published.

Dickens

The Age

	Dickens	The Age
1860–61	*Great Expectations* published in *All the Year Round.* Public readings become more fervent.	
1864–65	*Our Mutual Friend.* Severe shock of railway accident breaks his nerve and leads to decline in health and stability.	
1866		Publication of *Crime and Punishment.*
1867		Second Reform Bill extends suffrage to most wage earners, exclusive of rural laborers. Publication of *Das Kapital.*
1867–68	Immensely successful reading tour of the United States brings about exhaustion and near-collapse.	
1869	Begins The *Mystery of Edwin Drood.*	
1870	Ends public reading; received by the Queen; retires to Gad's Hill. Suffers a stroke and dies on June 9. Buried in Westminster Abbey on June 14. *Edwin Drood* left unfinished.	

Notes on the Editor and Contributors

CHARLES E. BECKWITH, Professor of English at California State College, Los Angeles, is a contributor to the forthcoming Oxford edition of the works of John Gay.

A. O. J. COCKSHUT, fellow of Hertford College, Oxford, is the author of *Anglican Attitudes* and *The Unbelievers,* a study of the religious controversies of the nineteenth century.

EARLE DAVIS, Chairman of the English Department at Kansas State University, has written various articles on Dickens, several textbooks and volumes of poetry, and *Vision Fugitive: Ezra Pound and Economics.*

SERGEI EISENSTEIN (1898–1948), director of *Potemkin* and *Ivan the Terrible,* was, like D. W. Griffith, one of the great innovators in film as art work.

JOHN GROSS, who has taught at the Universities of Cambridge and London and is now a freelance writer, has published an edition of Gissing's *New Grub Street,* a monograph on James Joyce, and *The Rise and Fall of the Man of Letters,* a study of the role of reviewers and reviewing in the nineteenth and early twentieth centuries in England.

JACK LINDSAY is a historian, novelist, poet, archaeologist, and critic, whose many books include lives of Bunyan, Cézanne, and Cleopatra, besides works on ancient alchemy and an edition of the poems of Marx and Engels for a forthcoming collection of their works.

The late WILLIAM H. MARSHALL was Professor of English at the University of North Carolina, Chapel Hill, and author of *The World of the Victorian Novel,* of which the earlier article here reprinted forms part of Chapter VII in modified form.

GEORGE ORWELL (1903–1950), whose work as a whole has been obscured by the fame of *Animal Farm* and *1984,* has now been represented in his full range by a four-volume collection of his essays, journalism, and letters.

GEORGE BERNARD SHAW (1856–1950), whose remark that *Little Dorrit* was a more seditious book than *Das Kapital* is characteristically excessive, was nevertheless early in his perception of the revolutionary thrust that lay beneath the sentiment and moralizing of Dickens.

G. ROBERT STANGE, Chairman of the English Department at Tufts University, is author of *Matthew Arnold: the Poet as Humanist* and numerous articles on nineteenth century literature.

TAYLOR STOEHR, Professor of Literature at the University of California at Santa Cruz, is a historian of nineteenth century culture who has written a number of articles on nineteenth century American figures and movements.

Selected Bibliography

Bodelson, C. A. "Some Notes on Dickens' Symbolism." *English Studies,* XL
(1959), 420–31. Asserts the greater importance of symbolic pattern—
exemplified in *A Tale of Two Cities* by contrasts of light and dark, recur-
rent color effects, journeys toward a catastrophic goal—than plot pattern,
an importance not recognized in Dickens's time, even by Dickens.

Brain, Russell. "Dickensian Diagnoses." In *Some Reflections on Genius.* New
York: J. B. Lippincott, Co., 1960. Praises Dickens's psychological insight,
chiefly shown in his treatment of Dr. Manette as a multiple personality
whose old identity is tied to the symbol of the shoemaker's bench, and who
can achieve his new or "real" self only when the old controlling symbol is
destroyed.

Collins, Philip. *Dickens and Crime.* London: Macmillan & Co., Ltd., 1962.
Contains no separate section on *A Tale of Two Cities,* but remarks *passim*
are of special interest, such as that the idea of showing the effects of live
burial came from Dickens's experience in visiting prisons, including American prisons, where he observed the deadly effects of solitary confinement
and imposed silence, and asked himself if ghosts were one of the terrors of
gaols.

Falconer, J. A. "Sources of *A Tale of Two Cities.*" *Modern Language Notes,*
XXXVI (1921), 1–10. Studies several borrowings and parallels from a
variety of sources, such as Mercier's *Tableau de Paris,* an anecdote from
Carlyle's *French Revolution,* and Scott's *Rokeby,* revealing something of
the range of threads from Dickens's reading that are woven into *A Tale of
Two Cities.*

Fielding, K. J. "Separation—and *A Tale of Two Cities.*" Chapter X of
Charles Dickens: A Critical Study. London: Longmans, Green, & Co., Ltd.,
1958. A brief but full narrative of Dickens's separation, his relations with
his wife's parents, and the beginning of *All the Year Round,* along with
some discussion of the novel which names Lucie as the central figure and
Dr. Manette, the imprisoned one who feels a compulsive need for action,
as the figure with whom Dickens feels the greatest identification.

Gregory, Michael. "Old Bailey Speech in *A Tale of Two Cities.*" *Review of
English Literature,* VI (1965), 42–55. A linguistic study, applying some

newly defined categories of speech to Darnay's first trial, attempting to show the appropriateness of the various forms to the various moments in the trial, hence Dickens's dramatic control on even so meticulous a level as "vocal and aural potential."

Jackson, T. A. "The *Tale of Two Cities.*" In *Charles Dickens: The Progress of a Radical.* New York: International Publishers, 1938. An offering of the "Marxist" Dickens which designates the adverse criticism of the time as bourgeois hostility contriving to let the story pass as a moral tale in which Carton's sacrifice redeems the horrors of the Revolution, whereas the real force of the story lies in Dickens's approach, "nearer than ever," to a positive assertion of revolution as man's only hope.

Johnson, Edgar. "The Tempest and the Ruined Garden." Chapter iii, Part IX, of *Charles Dickens: His Tragedy and Triumph.* 2 vols. New York: Simon and Schuster, Inc., 1952. A uniformly sensible survey of the book, scotching the biographical literalness of some criticism while acknowledging the characters and their situations as representative of various aspects of Dickens's emotional dilemma, which he expresses with "new and flaming power" even though in the book at large the themes of love and revolution do not satisfactorily mix, each tending to blur the other.

McMaster, R. D. "Dickens and the Horrific." *Dalhousie Review,* XXXVIII (1958), 18–28. Asserts that Dickens's obsession with ghastliness is constant and profound, part of the very fiber of his web. Points out as a source of the gossip at the well about the punishment of Monseigneur's murderer the torture and execution of Damiens, attempted murderer of Louis XV, as narrated in *The Terrific Register; or, a Record of Crimes, Judgments, Providences, and Calamities,* a sadistic journal read by Dickens as a boy.

Milley, H. J. "Wilkie Collins and *A Tale of Two Cities.*" *Modern Language Review,* XXXIV (1939), 525–34. Suggests that the French Revolution and Carlyle's book are not so influential as Collins's play about self-sacrifice, in which Dickens acted, *The Frozen Deep;* and his *Sister Rose,* a long tale of regeneration through self-sacrifice during the Revolution, which was first printed in *Household Words* in 1855.

Monod, Sylvère, "Dickens as Historical Novelist: *A Tale of Two Cities*" and "The Evolution of Dickens' Art in *Hard Times* and *A Tale of Two Cities.*" Sections iii and iv of Chapter XXV of *Dickens the Novelist.* Norman: University of Oklahoma Press, 1968. A shrewd weighing of Dickens's talents and equipment for historical fiction, found wanting in the larger application but excellent in the creation of atmosphere and emotion, though often with exaggeration, distortion, and rhetorical repetition, flaws which in turn are balanced by the book's firm and symmetrical construction.

Shannon, Edgar F. "The Dramatic Element in Dickens." *Sewanee Review,* XXI (1913), 277–86. An early study of the instinct for drama so strong in Dickens from the beginning, which contrasts the melodramatic treatment in *Oliver Twist* with the genuinely dramatic in *A Tale of Two Cities,* a far more artistic piece of work—indeed, Dickens's last great novel.

Wilson, Angus. *"A Tale of Two Cities."* In *The World of Charles Dickens.* New York: The Viking Press, 1970. Calls the work a "middle-brow" success, bought with the sacrifice of all Dickens's greatest gifts, which fails artistically to adjust the relationship between the domestic life of its characters and the Revolution, but which in its paring down had great importance as a preparation for *Great Expectations,* very likely his most perfect novel.

Zabel, Morton D. "The Revolutionarry Fate." Chapter iii, Part I, of *Craft and Character.* New York: The Viking Press, 1957. An extensive discussion of *A Tale of Two Cities* and its reception by various readers, its continuing significance despite its weaknesses, its timeliness as a warning to society, and its combination of tragic instinct and humane hope, generating a unique tone.